The
Death
of
Manolete

Illustrated

Barnaby Conrad

Copyright © 2007 Barnaby Conrad and Phoenix Books and Audio Inc.

ISBN: 1-59777-548-7

Originally published in hardcover: Boston: Houghton Mifflin, 1958.

Library of Congress Cataloging-In-Publication Data Available

Cover and book design by: Sonia Fiore
Jacket paintings by: the author

Printed in the United States of America

Phoenix Books
9465 Wilshire Boulevard, Suite 315
Beverly Hills, CA 90212

10 9 8 7 6 5 4 3

THIS IS MANUEL LAUREANO RODRÍGUEZ

CALLED
Manolete

THE GREATEST MATADOR OF MODERN TIMES

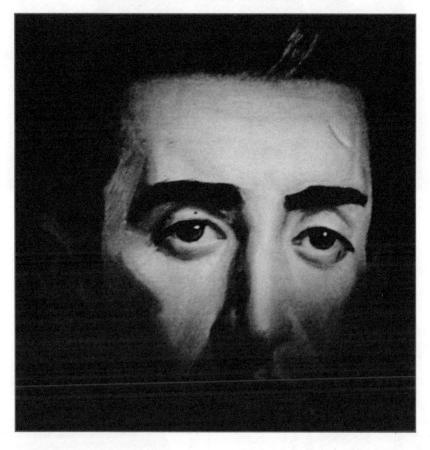

THIS IS ISLERO, OF MIURA

OUT OF THE COW ISLERA

BY THE BULL FORMALITO

HERE, IN THE TOWN OF LINARES,

THEY ARE GOING TO KILL EACH OTHER TODAY

The Death of Manolete

Illustrated

Barnaby Conrad

For Mary

Author's Note

This book is an attempt to recreate faithfully with words and photographs the day Manolete was killed. However, just as the pictures used to illustrate how Islero developed from a calf to a bull could not actually be of that very Miura, so not all the photographs of Manolete and Dominguín needed to tell the story were taken that fatal day. Enough photographs of the actual corrida in Linares simply do not exist; therefore some supplementary photographs taken on other days had to be used.

B.C.

M ANUEL LAUREANO RODRÍGUEZ Y SÁNCHEZ was born in Córdoba on July 4, 1917, the year the immortals of the ring, Joselito and Belmonte, had their most competitive and glorious season. Manuel's mother was the widow of the matador Lagartijo Chico before she married Manuel's father.

Manuel's father was a fairly successful though far from great matador who used the name Manolete as a *nom de taureau* as had his father before him. The first Manolete had a brief career as a banderillero before retiring to the safer profession of butcher; he had been overshadowed by his famous brother "Pepete."

José Rodríguez, called "Pepete," was large and ungraceful in the arena, but he was considered one of the bravest men who ever confronted a bull. Rather than ever having to conquer any fear, he simply did not recognize what that emotion was. Once when a rival had outdone him in the capework of the *quites*, Pepete went out determined to do anything to triumph. When the bull's horns pulled the cape from his hands, Pepete snatched a bandanna from the pocket of his chaquetilla and gave the animal four hair-raising passes with no more protection than that small cloth.

In 1862, when Pepete was 38 years old, he signed for a corrida in Madrid and was scheduled to kill the celebrated Miura bull Jocinero. Jocinero had a fearsome reputation, being large and almost six years old, and having been at stud for some time because of the ferocity he displayed on the ranch. But Pepete went into this fight with the same

sang-froid as any other encounter. Though he was crisscrossed with scars, his courage had never diminished and he was at the peak of his career. He did his opening capework, received great applause for the closeness with which he worked, and then retired for a

moment behind the fence to talk to a friend in the first row. It was the time for the picadors and Jocinero charged hard at the first horse. The animal went down and the picador was spilled directly in front of the bull's horns. Pepete whirled when he heard the crowd scream, and with the cape still folded over his arm, he leaped over the fence between the bull and the fallen picador.

Pepete managed to distract the animal away from the picador, but in doing so he was taken off balance and in a dangerous area. The right horn caught him, and he was lifted high

up in the air. He managed to grab the horn with his powerful hands, and pushed himself off and away from the animal's head. But when he fell to the ground, the bull attacked hard and succeeded in slightly wounding him twice. The third time the horn went straight into and through his heart.

The historian Cossío reports it this way: "Once the bull had left him, Pepete managed to get to his feet with no help. Automatically, he dusted the sand off his pants with his right hand, and then, with an unbelievable force of will holding him perfectly erect, he walked unaided straight to the caudrilla gate where he fell, striking his head on the stirrup board and cutting his forehead. Blood suddenly gushed from his chest in torrents, and though they rushed him to the infirmary, he was dead three minutes after the tossing. They say he asked the doctors in a calm voice before dying: 'Is it anything?' He was the second matador ever to die in the Madrid arena."

So little Manuel grew up in the shadow of the legendary Pepete, his great-uncle. The son, grandson, nephew and great-nephew of toreros, Manuel grew up with no interest at all in the bulls at first. His father took him to a bullfight when he

4

was just six. "I remember I hated the horse part," Manolete recalled years later, "and my father chided me."

Delicate and sickly, having almost died of pneumonia when he was two, little Manuel was interested only in painting and reading. He stayed so much indoors and clung so tightly to his mother's apron strings that his sisters and other children used to tease him. "I was a mother's boy in the worst degree," he told me once.

When he was six, his father died, broke and sick. The senior Manuel Rodríguez had had a bad time of it in the last years; his vision had always been bad, but toward the end he was virtually blind. He insisted on trying to fight, even when he saw the image of two bulls charging him. One day he even wore his glasses into the ring, but the sight of a matador with spectacles was too ridiculous for the crowd to take and he was forced to retire. Shortly afterward he died.

Young Manuel was known around the town of Córdoba as a thin, melancholy boy who wandered around the streets after school lost in thought. He rarely joined in other boys' games of soccer or playing at bullfighting.

One day he saw Juan Belmonte arrive at Córdoba and he watched the cheering crowd that greeted the greatest of matadors at the hotel. He was excited. A man near him scoffed: "Belmonte's just like Sevillano—we've produced better toreros here in Córdoba—men like Machaquito and Guerrita and even your father."

Manolete was filled with a sudden great pride. Shortly thereafter he announced to his mother that he was going to be a torero. She was dismayed. Her name was Angustias: "anguishes." Very carefully, after her second husband's death, she had hidden everything to do with bullfighting in the house; all the posters, photographs, and costumes. She had hoped and prayed that he

6

would never be a victim of "the little worm of la afición" that had inflicted so many others in the family.

But now it had happened, happened suddenly and irrevocably. From the time he was about eleven, nothing else mattered much except the bulls. Perhaps it was seeing the idolatry accorded Belmonte. Perhaps it was because he was starting to become a man and had just begun to realize that fighting bulls was simply what men in his family were supposed to do. Perhaps he was suddenly aware of how very poor they were and how much his mother and sisters suffered because of it.

In any event, he began training with the other aspirants around the neighborhood; training, that is, with a tattered cape and a boy charging with a pair of s l a u g h t e r h o u s e horns held in front of him. One of the older boys was usually patient with the skinny newcomer and showed him all the passes that the other youths had known for years. His name was Guillermo, and a few years later, he was to vie up his own career as a torero to serve as a sword handler to Manolete until the day he died.

Young Manuel was very bad at this business of playing at bullfighting. He was gawky, awkward, and when he tried the spinning graceful passes made so popular by the big stars of that season, Chicuelo and Lalanda, the others laughed at him. The only thing he did well and with style was to kill the mechanical bull. This consisted of a pair of horns mounted on a bicycle wheel, plus a length of pipe mounted between where the shoulder blades would be on a real bull. But each time Manuel would fling himself over the right horn and sink the sword into the pipe as though it were a charging Miura that had to be liquidated.

Finally the time came when he had his first chance to try his skill with real animals. It was at the Florentino Sotomayor ranch in back of Córdoba and they were holding a "tentadero," the time when the wild heifers are tested for bravery. It so happened that the great bullfighting critic Corrochano from the Madrid "ABC" happened to be visiting the ranch that day. This is what he wrote the next day in the newspaper:

"I have just seen the son of Manolete, the matador from Córdoba, fight for the first time. The boy—still a child, really, in knee pants—performed with style and taste.... With the muleta in the left hand, he passed the heifer back and forth as many times as he felt like it, his feet nailed to the ground, stretching his arm out to the fullest, not waving it around like a flag the way some do, but rather leading the animal along in its folds just right. It all seemed quite perfect to me. Then young Manolete—I assume that is what he is to be called— let down a bit, lost his animal to its querencia near the exit gate, and when he went in that dangerous terrain after her, she swung around abruptly and caught him in the

groin with one horn. Someone saw right away that he was bleeding and dragged him behind a burladero. Luckily, it was just a scratch, but in a dangerous place. He withstood the first aid very bravely, without a murmur, and when it was bandaged and someone offered him a lift back to Córdoba, he replied very solemnly: 'I've come with my friends, and I wish to return with them. This happening is of no importance.'"

Manolete became somewhat of a hero among his friends. What had happened out there with the heifer to so transform him? Somehow in that very first encounter he displayed some of the genius that was later to make him immortal in the annals of tauromachy.

The road ahead looked easy now. He went to every "tentadero" he could, but with less success than the first time. He kept trying, but he could not find that magic formula that Corrochano had so admired. By the time he was fifteen, he was fighting in minor village fair fights and "nocturnals" in and around

Córdoba, but often he provided the comic relief. The stiffness of the lanky boy's body and the sadness of his face which were later to become regal grace, dignity and disdain now just caused audiences to laugh.

When he was sixteen, he joined "Los Califas," a comic bull-fighting group that toured around the country giving their tawdry exhibitions. Manolete, as he was being billed now, was supposed to come on after the clowns had finished their antics with a calf and fight a bull in a serious fashion; however, the crowd's laughter frequently overlapped.

"He has a face that's as dreary as a third-class funeral on a rainy day," said one critic, "and his body is like an undriven nail."

Nevertheless, they couldn't laugh at the way the boy killed. His capework was bad, but when he "went in" with the sword, the animals dropped as though they'd been poleaxed. Mainly because of this one skill, he wangled himself a fight in Madrid when he was seventeen. All Manuel's hopes were pinned on his performance here in the most important city in the world for a torero. It started off badly when the billboards got his name wrong, writing "Angel Rodríguez *Manolete*." Here is what the newspapers said the next day:

El Liberal: "Two Mexicans and two Spaniards on the card. None of them did anything worth discussing. It's enough to say that when they weren't being tossed in the air, they were being booed for their deplorable performances.

El Debate: "Angel Rodríguez *Manolete* is very green with the cape and muleta but he killed with impeccable style and results."

Informaciones: "Angel Rodíguez *Manolete*... is a poor unknowing devil who hasn't the faintest idea

what a muleta and cape are for, nor does he even know how to hold them properly. On the other hand, he kills superbly.... But killing isn't everything: to be a torero you have to know a bit more than how to supply the butcher with goods."

Not long afterward, the decisive thing in Manolete's career took place. José Flores Camará happened to see him perform. Camará was once a good but not great matador who had long since retired when he found out that he didn't have the necessary guts to reach the top. When he saw Manolete in the ring, he somehow saw beyond what the boy was to what he could someday become.

He saw instantly that the boy was doing the wrong kind of passes for his build and personality. He saw that it was ignorance of terrains that was causing the boy to be tossed all the time.

But he also saw that Manolete had tremendous courage. He saw that he killed better than anyone he had ever seen, killed in the old-fashioned dangerous, stylish, straight-over-the-right-horn, up-to-the-hilt school of killing that had all but disappeared from the arenas.

Camará signed up Manolete, and as his manager he began to remake him. He took him out on the ranches with the calves and started teaching him about bullfighting from scratch.

He wouldn't permit him to do any of the fancy twirling passes that were so in vogue and which Manolete had been trying to do. Only the classic passes—the verónica and the half-verónica with the capote; right and left-handed naturals, the Pass of Death, and the chest pass with the muleta.

The remaking of Manolete was interrupted when Manolete had to do two years of military service. But Camará was in no great rush; it was good for the boy to fill out and strengthen his frail frame a bit. And Camará saw to it that he kept up his training by doing benefit corridas for the soldiers.

When he got out in 1938, Camará decided to launch his protégé.

Manolete was an instant hit.

At first Camará kept him in the small towns, but when he saw what an impression the new style was making on audiences, he took him into Sevilla and Madrid.

People had simply never seen a man stand there with such dignity and serenity while half a ton of bull charged.

This man would plant his feet on the ground and not move them back an inch as the horns sliced a few inches by his legs time after time.

Contrary to the normal instinct to bend over at the waist and jump back out of the way of danger, Manolete would make himself stand absolutely straight. When he did the Pass of Death, only his head would turn calmly as his heavy-lidded eyes watched the horns cut by his chest.

"Toro-o-o-o—" he would call in his deep Cordovan accent, and then all the while death came at him and was deceived into missing him, his feet would remain where he had placed them at the beginning of the pass.

He took "the alternative" from Marcial Lalanda and graduated to the status of full matador in July, 1939, in a ceremony in Sevilla and then confirmed it in Madrid that October. The same critics who had ridiculed him before were now saying: "Never has

there been such a torero—never has there been such elegance and dignified grace in the history of bullfighting!" He was awarded ears at first, then ears and tail, and finally they had to create a new award for him—a hoof. When he surpassed even that performance, there was nothing else to do but grant two hooves!

And always behind the fence was the little man in the dark glasses saying: "Be careful, Manolo, this one is dangerous—he doesn't see well with his right horn"—or: "Fight him over there across the ring, Manolo, he charges easier there." Camará had made a genius out of a clown.

Antonio Diaz-Cañabate writes in *The Magic World of the Bullfighter* about how the transformation from the youth of the comic bullfights to the idol of Spain had come about:

"His physical appearance was not at that time any great asset to him, for his style lacked those qualities of calm serenity, aplomb, and even majesty which in the near future were to become the foundations of his triumph. He had not yet reached his full stature as a man, and still less so as a torero. But when later he achieved them both, he no longer gave the impression that he was lacking in grace. On the contrary, his considerable height and his long arms became the advantages upon which his artistry was solidly founded."*

In a recent letter I received from Lael Tucker Wertenbaker, she writes wonderfully well of the beautiful ugliness of Manolete and Belmonte:

* *London: Burke Publishing Co., Ltd*

"Their very ugliness, of course, did contribute to their arrogance and to the feeling one had that these men were not crowd-pleasers but self-pleasers (or conquerors), who stood out there fighting bulls for the sake of lonely triumphs. It doesn't matter how well-based this feeling is—not Arruza nor Luis Miguel Dominguín nor Ordóñez ever gave the same sensation. They were too handsome, too superbly and fittingly accoutered, too graceful in the moments between, when they stood against fences or sauntered in safety. The sense—not the reality—of great theatre, of matinee, was inescapably there in them. But with Belmonte and Manolete there was no theatre, no beauty—(or it was most imperfect, as if Hamlet came on as a fat man)—until bull and matador established their direct relationship. Then, when it came, there was a Moment of Miracle. I saw this with Manolete. That pop-eyed, chinless, badly bodied, painfully and barely dignified man, whose suits of lights never quite fit however they were tailored, shambling into the arena with arrogance as wrinkled as his pants legs. And then—when he went still and challenged the bull—it was almost enough, that single moment...beauty was created from clay in front of your eyes in a single instant. The impact varied with the character and appreciations of the beholder, but it couldn't fail to touch with triumph anyone who saw it."

And so he went to the top, and he remained there for eight years, the most popular and highest paid matador in the world.

It had been hard to get to the top, but it was harder to stay there. He had to put forth his best every time he entered the arena, and took incredible chances to maintain his position of El Número Uno. There were plenty of tossings and twelve serious gorings. But he kept climbing higher with each season, fighting more corridas, getting higher prices. In 1944, he performed in ninety-two corridas in a six-month season and was indisputably Spain's greatest hero. He couldn't walk down the street in any town without crowds gathering and swarming around him. Best-selling books were written about him, a song called "Manolete" was and still is one of

the most popular of pasodobles, statues were erected to him, and a liqueur that changed its name to "Anís Manolete" became popular overnight. Famous people of all nationalities sought his friendship and to be invited to the ceremony of watching him don the suit of lights was tantamount to an interview at the Castel Gandolfo.

It wasn't just that he was the best torero of the day; he was the embodiment of everything Spanish. He was what every Spaniard aspired to be, he was the gallant, arrogant, courageous Spaniard of pre-Armada days. Diaz-Cañabate writes:

"Watching him perform, it was the personality of the man that struck one, a personality that was extraordinarily attractive and was the real secret of his art. He possessed a presence which bordered on the arrogant and an elegance that was compelling, not only when he was actually facing the bull itself, but also from the moment he stepped into the arena. To see him march around after a successful faena, acknowledging the plaudits of the crowd, was a spectacle in itself. But Manolete possessed other qualities as well and in high degree—a sense of honor, a consciousness of his responsibilities and a transparent courage. He was by nature a melancholy man, and this sadness was plainly reflected in his art. But it was the sadness of an artist, a sadness tinged with languor, and a sadness against which his artistry stood out in high relief in a manner that was quite extraordinary."*

Ugly in photographs, cold and hard in the bull ring, away from bullfighting he was a gentle, modest and charming companion.

But he had few close friends of either sex because, as he told me

* *The Magic World of the Bullfighter.*

once: "I never know whether they like Manuel Rodríguez or only Manolete."

I remember chiding a titled woman who was hopelessly in love with Manolete: "You only love him because he's the top matador in the world." And she retorted so well: "But of course! A man is what he does—and how he does it—and why he does it. If he were a bricklayer—or a banker—he would not be Manolete."

In December, 1945, he went to Mexico for the most arduous ordeal a torero ever had to face. For years the Mexicans had been reading about the fabulous Manolete. He came billed as the world's greatest bullfighter and the Mexicans were determined to make him prove it. Charging the highest prices ever charged by any matador, he filled El Toreo plaza, and people thought they

were lucky to get a ticket on the sombra side for one hundred American dollars. I met one American who paid $500 for a single first row barrera seat and said afterward: "It was worth every penny."

For Manolete did not let his audience, his country, or even his press agents down. He took Mexico as no other Spanish bullfighter had ever done. He was carried out badly gored in that first fight, but not before he had shown Mexico City why he was called "El Monstruo"—the monster of matadors.

He fought thirty-one times more in Mexico, Columbia, Venezuela, and Peru and left them begging for more at any price. He returned to Spain, fought only one corrida in Madrid, and then returned in the fall of 1946 for another whirlwind season in Mexico. This time he fought seventeen corridas in Mexico alone, with greater success than the year before. He was the indisputable king of the world of tauromachy.

But he was tired—scarred and terribly tired. He was worried about his eyesight also. Diaz-Cañabate reports:

"A few hours before a corrida of great importance to him, Manolete himself raised the subject.

"'I'm afraid I've inherited this affliction from my parents,' he said.

"'My mother was treated by the best specialists in Barcelona and Madrid, but without success. At the beginning of each season, when I get into the arena, I feel this pricking behind my eyes and I ask myself—is it just dust, or can it be the effects of fear? To-day, for example, my eyes are in poor shape and irritate horribly. What do you think it can be? There's certainly no dust in this room, so it must be fear—that fear which grips you by the entrails and never lets go.'

"'I expect it's only an eyelash that's got under the lid. Let me look. Yes—there you are, there is one!' replied his friend and at once removed the offending hair.

"'Thank you,' said Manolete with a smile. 'And now—what about the fear? Can you remove that with the same ease?'"

He began to think about retiring. After his last great fight in Mexico City, Manolete was feted at a banquet before leaving for

Spain. At his left, they seated Joselillo.

He was a twenty-two-year-old Mexican novillero who had become somewhat of a sensation overnight with his great bravery and style. He worshiped Manolete and had asked to be allowed to sit by him.

During the meal, Manolete said abruptly: "I've had a good season. I think I will get out now. For good."

"We would all get out," Joselillo answered, "if we had any sense."

(Joselillo was to be killed exactly one month to the day after Manolete, ironically enough, while executing a pass named after his idol—the manoletina.)

When Manolete returned to Spain, he announced his intentions of not fighting that year and perhaps never again. He just wanted to rest, he told the newspapermen. Rest, rest, rest on his newly acquired 13,000,000-peseta ranch near Córdoba and raise bulls for younger men to test their manhood on.

Then the hue and cry started. They would not let him go so easily. They would murder him first. Instead of rejoicing that a Spaniard had comported himself so gloriously in Latin America, the press attacked him. He was accused of being un-Spanish for having ignored an anti-Mexican compact urged by the unions; he was charged with having had the horns of his bulls filed and of only fighting the smallest animals available; and it was declared that the real reason he was retiring was that he knew he was slipping and that he was afraid to compete alongside of Dominguín.

Here was the real instigator: Luis Miguel Conzález *Dominguín*, 21, arrogant, cocky, handsome, skillful, ambitious. Born of a matador father, both his older brothers matadors, Luis Miguel had begun his career when he was ten years old.

When still a child, he had a successful tour of Latin America as a becerrista, a calf fighter. For over ten years, he'd been perfecting his great talents. By the time he was 21, he was not just a good-looking athlete; he was a complete, versatile, cool veteran matador.

Now his ambitious father, ex-matador Domingo González, decided that his son was ready to be proclaimed the greatest bull-fighter in the world. And how best to prove that Luis Miguel was the Número Uno? By competing with and showing up the acknowledged maestro. But how to induce Manolete to come out of the retirement he so recently had retreated to?

Diaz-Cañabate tells how it was accomplished in *The Magic World of the Bullfighter*:

"In the 1947 season, Luis Miguel was rather badly wounded by a bull. One day, while he was convalescing though still in bed, he rang up the chief of the bullfighting section of one of the Madrid broadcasting stations.

"'I should very much like to give a talk on the current state of affairs in the world of tauromachy,' he told him. 'What I have to say is, I think, of interest, but I should like to broadcast it myself, so that there can be no misunderstanding. Would it be possible for me to speak from my bed?'

"'Certainly. We will simply record you talk on a wire recorder.'

"'Excellent! When would you be prepared to do so?'

"'At any time that suits your convenience.'

"'To-morrow?'

"'Yes—to-morrow by all means.'

"The next day thousands of people were astonished to hear a more or less extempore talk by Luis Miguel. The gist of what he said was as follows: 'At the present moment two *toreros* are competing for

the privilege of being regarded as the best *torero* of the age. One is Manolete, the other Carlos Arruza. The latter does not interest me, for I regard his claim for consideration to be quite unjustified. The case for Manolete is quite different. For reasons which are beyond my control, I am unable to perform, as I should like to do, in the same *corridas* with him. I am anxious to furnish proof that I am a better *torero* than he and that I can unseat him from the pedestal on which public opinion has placed him and which he now claims as his right. It is my intention to prove my superiority in the only way open to me—in the ring and face to face with the *toros*. The moment I am given the chance, I will prove that I am the best of them all.'

"The timing of Luis Miguel's bombshell was admirable. Manolete at the moment was at the height of his popularity and had acquired an enormous fortune, thanks to fees greater than any that had ever before been paid to any *torero*. On the other hand, the public, as insatiable as ever, was forever demanding more and more of him. Manolete was doing his utmost to satisfy his public, but the latter demanded superhuman exhibitions, and Manolete was only mortal—not a god. It was, then, inevitable that in some *corridas* he should disappoint his admirers, while the public screamed that it hadn't been given its money's worth. Fickle and cruel, it hooted and whistled at the man who shortly before had earned its rapturous adulation.

"Luis Miguel's challenge, therefore, was acclaimed with unholy glee. There's nothing that the masses in general—and the arena masses in particular—adore more than a clash of rivals. Manolete, then, was no longer the undisputed monarch of the arena, they told themselves; he had a rival, and this rivalry would without a doubt produce some magnificent *corridas*, palpitating with passion and emotion. Bravo! *Viva* Luis Miguel! shouted some, while for others the challenge which he had just hurled forth merely confirmed their opinion that Luis Miguel was a pretentious and vainglorious braggart.

"But whichever way you looked at it, the challenge caused a very considerable sensation in bull-fighting circles—and that was just what Luis Miguel was aiming at, while his father, adroit as ever as a producer, remained hidden behind the scenes. A *torero* but recently grievously wounded hurls from his bed of convalescence a defiant and theatrical challenge to the idol of the arena, the man who, by common consent, reigned supreme in the art of tauro-machy. It cannot be denied that there was a measure of grandeur in the gesture; and when, in addition, it is realized that the cunningly calculated insolence of his demeanour had in it everything that was required to incite the masses, it will readily be seen that his action was bound, eventually, to bear fruit. As for Domingo González, when people pointed out to him the dangers inherent in this rivalry to which young Luis Miguel's act had given birth, he merely smiled and said nothing.

"At first Manolete himself, with a pretence of disdain for the bombast of his young rival, ignored the whole issue. That he did not immediately take up the challenge—a passivity which left Luis Miguel unmoved—did not in the least mean that both he and his advisers were not most anxious to accept it. The truth is that, fundamentally, Manolete had great need of a challenge of this kind and had, therefore, no option but to accept it. It was thus not very long before Luis Miguel achieved his ends.

"The clash between the two great *diestros* was arranged for the beginning of August. It was something which I would not have missed for anything in the world. As it was to take place in Vitoria, I left Madrid by car the day before, in company with Luis Miguel. The latter was in high fettle, completely at his ease, rather loquacious and disposed to jest and joke. We reached Vitoria in time for dinner.

"Vitoria is a very ecclesiastical city, steeped in patriarchal tradition and in no sense a centre of tauromachy. Indeed, the atmosphere of the arena was something quite foreign to it, and *corridas* in Vitoria were events of rare occurrence. Nevertheless, on that night the air in the streets and in every little café was charged with the scent of bulls. The two *toreros*, and which of them would triumph, were the sole topics of argument and conversation. The town, too, was obviously full of outsiders, particularly visitors from Madrid, for the *aficionados* had hastened from far and wide to be present at this first clash between the two great masters of their art....

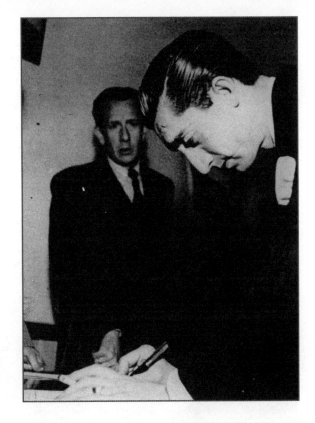

"The *corrida* was a great triumph for Luis Miguel. Manolete was gjven a hostile reception by several sections of the public, and particularly by a group of *aficionados* who had come specially from Bilbao. These latter had been incensed by the financial demands of Manolete's *apoderado*, which had been so high that they had precluded the possibility of engaging Manolete for the Bilbao Fiesta—a *fiesta* of very particular interest on account of the exceptionally large and massive *toros* used at it. The public attributed these excessive demands to a fear on Manolete's part to face these very formidable beasts. Manolete was quite out of his depth in the face of the Bilbao *aficionados'* violent hostility, which the attitude of the rest of the crowd did nothing to counteract. Indeed, on the whole, the audience was very hard on him, and this, of course, was all to the advantage of Luis Miguel, who was warmly encouraged and applauded by all."

And so Manolete, by popular demand, found himself having to confront Luis Miguel again. He signed to meet him in San Sebastian on August 16 and again in Linares on the 28th. In

34

between there would be easier corridas in Toledo, Gijón, and Santander against familiar and uninspired competition. But still it would be a grueling campaign, for the great Manolete could never coast; with his reputation and charging the fantastic prices he did he had to fight every corrida as though it were his first time in the Madrid ring.

He said goodbye to his mistress, Antoñita Bronchalo, who was going to the beach resort of Lanjarón. She was a pretty and vivacious girl who under the name of Lupe Sino had made a few movies in Spain. Diaz-Cañabate tells how she and Manolete had met for the first time:

"I cannot claim to have been one of his intimate friends. We met perhaps five or six times in all; and in any case it was not easy to get to know him, for he was besieged on all sides by people clamouring to gain his exclusive attention. I was, however, witness of an episode which had a large influence on his life, and not an entirely happy one. I was one of a group of friends who had the habit of dining together once a month, with each of us taking it in turn to be the host and the Amphytrion of the moment having the right to invite a guest or two, who were not members of our particular little circle. So it came about that one of these outside guests turned out to be Manolete, and as luck would have it, I was his neighbour at table. Also as luck would have it, opposite us were three young women, one of whom was very pretty, distractingly attractive. She was gay, jolly and filled with carefree abandon. As may well be imagined, she made a dead set at Manolete, who responded but vaguely and mostly in monosyllables…. Faced with so paltry a response, the young maiden got bored and stopped talking. Manolete took advantage of the hiatus to lean over close to my ear.

"'Who's that?' he whispered.

"'I don't know. But she's rather pretty, isn't she?'

"'What d'you mean—rather pretty? Why—she's the most beautiful woman in the world!'

"We exchanged these remarks in a low voice, and with rather an air of mystery. The young woman, of course, noticed it, and intervened at once.

"'What are you two whispering about? It's not done, you know. If you don't talk in an ordinary voice, I'll think you're saying something nasty.'

"Manolete screwed up his courage.

"'We were, indeed, talking about you, but not to say anything nasty; quite the contrary, I assure you.'

"'Well, first of all, tell me this—why this formality of address? I am not an old woman, as far as I know. Come on— loosen up a bit! Pay me some compliments! I adore being paid compliments!'

"Manolete remained tongue-tied, and the young woman returned to the charge.

"'Have you suddenly become dumb?'

"'I said that you were very pretty.'

"'Is that all?'

"'Isn't that enough?'

"'It's very little. People are always telling me I'm very pretty.'

"'I'm quite sure they are! But to a really beautiful woman one only says it when one's heart is full.'

"'Aha! That's better! Carry on!'

"But Manolete once more fell silent.

"'What a disappointment!' continued the young woman. 'Such a magnificent *torero* and—oh dear! such a dull man!'

"Scarcely had she said this than she gave a little cry, and a spasm of anguish crossed her face.

"'What's the matter?' asked Manolete.

"'Matter? Oh nothing—nothing at all! Except that you're not only a dull man, but also a clumsy brute into the bargain!'

"It was some minutes before I found out what had happened. Manolete had stretched out his leg until it touched that of the young woman. It may have been quite involuntary on his part, or he may have been trying to make her keep quiet. Be that as it may, he did it all so clumsily that a precious stocking was irretrievably ruined. When the party broke up, I heard that last bit of dialogue. It was the young woman saying to her gallant:

"'Don't forget—I shall expect you to-morrow; and above all, don't forget the dozen pairs of stockings you've promised me!'

"It was this same woman whom we saw arrive prostrate with grief at the hospital on the night that Manolete died. She had been the sole love of his life—perhaps even his only adventure in the lists of love."*

* The Magic World of the Bullfighter.

Antoñita gave up her career, such as it was, when she met Manolete and for three years she devoted herself to being with him. When he took her to Latin America with him on the last trip, people were sure they were going to be married, but it never came off. For some time Manolete had been drinking heavily, and many of his friends claimed that it was because of difficulties in their relationship.

In San Sebastían the great Mexican matador, Carlos Arruza, came to see Manolete before the fight. Originally, Arruza and Manolete, the greatest of rivals in the ring in the years of 1944 and 1946, had been enemies out of it. But one day in Valencia in 1945 they became the best of friends. Arruza tells about it in his autobiography *My Life as a Matador*:

"The impresario organized a party in the back part of the bullring, in the courtyard by the corrals, and the three matadors were invited as guests of honor. Deliberately, diabolically, they seated Manolete and me next to each other. I guess they just wanted to see the fireworks when the two enemies got together. At the beginning everything was serious, very cold, and completely silent. I nodded to him, however, and he nodded back. This, considering our past salutations, was practically the equivalent to an affectionate embrace.

"Then something happened. I don't know even now how we started. It was something simple like 'They call this food?'—but it broke the ice, and all of a sudden Manolete and I were talking.

"'You missed a fine opportunity to let me get killed off there in Sevilla,' he said laconically. 'I've wanted to thank you for not doing it.'

"'What would I do for a rival then?' I joked back off-handedly. 'I need the stimulus of the little competition you give me.'

"Then I saw something I thought was impossible. His mouth widened and he gave a low rumbling noise. Manolete was laughing! Then we began, and we talked and laughed steadily all through the meal and stayed on afterwards for another hour. We would have stayed all afternoon but we both had fights in other cities, and so after a warm handshake we said good-bye until our next fight together.

"That was how I began to know Manolete, the other Manolete, the charming, friendly, humorous one who existed only away from the plaza de toros. I had never met anyone whom I liked and admired so much as this man to whom bullfighting was a religion."

Part of the reason that Luis Miguel Domínguín had been catapulted into the position of challenging Manolete's throne in 1947 was the fact that Arruza was not allowed to perform in Spain because of the new boycott against Mexican matadors. The public desperately needed a rival for "El Monstruo," and since Arruza was out of the running they would make a hero out of Domínguín. They went to the plazas now to boo Manolete and to cheer Domínguín; nothing is so intolerable to the public as the continued success of any performer.

Arruza tells about the San Sebastián corrida:

"I had two corridas signed for the 27th and 28th of August in the plaza of Dax in France, so we set out from Sevilla in the station wagon and on the way stopped at San Sebastián, where the fair was on in full swing. Manolete was fighting, and I went to see him in the morning.

"To tell the truth, I was shocked by his physical state. He had been out on the town all night 'de juerga,' and I wondered how he could possibly fight that afternoon. The Spanish public had been brutal to him for over a year now, even though he had just returned from the most sensational season in Mexico and Latin America that any matador had ever enjoyed. He was fighting as well as he ever had, but after a while audiences became infuriated by perfection. They kept demanding more and more of him with every fight. Out of boredom they now wanted to destroy their once beloved idol. Manolete was too sincere an artist not to suffer under this treatment. I was worried, seeing his face even more tragic than ever and knowing of his present bitterness toward life because of personal and professional reasons. He was just thirty but he looked forty-five.

"I decided to stay for the fight, and Manolo did me the honor of asking me to watch it from down in the passageway. Once out in the ring, he quickly dispelled any fears I had about what shape he was in by putting up a highly capable demonstration, if not one of his really great ones. But he did many wonderful things that day, things that only another torero could truly appreciate, that the crowd didn't even deign to applaud.

"As he came over to the fence to change muletas I exclaimed, 'Carai, Manolo, what do they want!'

"'I know very well what they want,' he said enigmatically, 'and one of these afternoons I just might give it to them to keep the bastards happy.'

"They took a photo of us in the cuadrilla gate, the last together. Then we said good-bye warmly, but with what seemed to me a certain sadness and nostalgia for the great days we had shared that would never come again. As he climbed into his car, still dressed in his suit of lights, he turned and with that hint of tragic

smile that could break your heart he said, 'Make them applaud their hands off in France, compadre.'

"And then he set off, for he had engagements to fulfill. One special engagement was awaiting him, one terrible rendezvous in Linares, from which he wasn't to return, and he hurried off to keep it, almost eagerly, it seems to me now in retrospect."

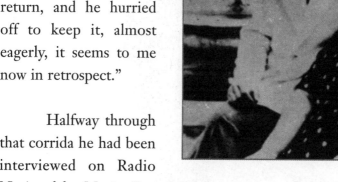

Halfway through that corrida he had been interviewed on Radio Nacional by Matías Prat. Manolete said simply: "They're asking more than I can give. I only want to say one thing: I am very anxious for this season to end...."

After the corrida he saw his mother, who was spending the summer in San Sebastián. In a newspaper, José Luis de Córdoba quoted Doña Angustias a few days after Manolete's death:

"The visit was short. Manolo sat down as though very tired. He asked for a glass of cold wine. I said to him: 'My son, we see you so seldom!' and he answered: 'Mother, I am not the child I once was. I have to fight bulls. And the friends and the engagements don't leave time for anything....' We didn't talk much more. Then he stood up. He kissed me. The last kiss! Just before he left I said: 'Manolo, you look very rundown. Take care of yourself, son, take care of yourself!' And then he left forever, oh God!"

On Wednesday, August 27, Manolete set out from Madrid for Linares. His number two sword boy, Chimo, reported how Manolete spent his last night in a letter written to Antonio de la Villa five days later:

"My matador, may he rest in peace, went to fight in Linares with enthusiasm. It was the first corrida of the season for him in Andaluclía and you know how much toreros want to please the aficionados there, especially those near Córdoba and Sevilla, which are the ones that have the power to bestow or remove fame.

"For Manolete the Miura bulls were no worry at all since he'd had some of his best days with them. Balañá, who was the impresario of Linares, had bought two corridas, one from Samuel Brothers and the other from Miura. Manolo requested the Miuras.

"And they try to say there's nothing to superstition! On the 21st of August Balañá arranged the fight, number 21 was the hotel room number in Linares, Manolete had fought 21 fights already this season, and 21 was the brand on Islero, the assassin of poor Manolo. These are forewarnings that never leave one.

"I left Madrid with the cuadrilla in order to have everything ready in Linares. Manolo, with Guillermo, Camará and his friend Bellón, left Madrid at nightfall in his car (whose license plate began with '21.')

"He ate dinner in Manzanares with great relish—you know how he loved to eat—and afterwards he sat around listening to some flamenco records and chatting with a friend of his from Manzanares who kept begging him to fight there. The friend began flattering Camará to get him to go for the idea, and to convince him, he took out his checkbook, saying to Manolo, 'You put in the amount, any amount, and I'll sign it.' But Manolete begged off, saying he had twenty fights in a row and he couldn't accept.

46

"Manolete arrived at the Hotel Cervantes around 12:30 that night. There awaited him Domecq, Antonio Cañero, Bernardo, Carnicerito, and other friends. They stayed up talking and joking until nearly two in the morning. They didn't talk about bulls or anything unpleasant, only about things of the country, horses, and trips."

The next morning, the fair of San Agustín, patron saint of the mining town, was going full blast. There was much guitar playing, lots of "cante jondo," and many a bottle of manzanilla emptied.

The girls vied with each other to see who could dance the best bulería or sevillana, and the castanets sounded like machine gun fire in the streets.

The whole town was keyed up by the corrida they were going to see today. There were almost nine thousand seats in the plaza de toros but these had been sold out long ago at astronomic figures, and now the public had to do battle with the scalpers.

At the sidewalk cafés, people discussed nothing else but the burning question—who would do better, Manolete or Dominguín? People had come from Sevilla and Córdoba and from as far as Madrid and Barcelona. Many felt that the young challenger would show up the maestro.

"He's young, he has class, variety. He'll give old Big Nose the bath."

"Maybe he will," said some of the experts, "maybe he will if he draws a good bull. But on the other hand, remember that when he wants to, Manolete can handle any bull in the world."

"But he hates Miuras," argued the dominguinistas.

And the manoletistas had to admit that it looked as though this were true. In his eight years as a full matador he had killed more than 1200 bulls, but only 14 of these were Miuras. (As opposed to 92 from the ranch of Antonio Pérez, 48 from Murube, 40 from Albaserrada, and so forth.) And 14 is a small number when one considers the 88 Miuras Joselito killed before his death at the age of twenty-five or the 76 which Belmonte had to his credit when he retired in 1972. He had

had some great afternoons with Miuras, as his sword handler stated, being awarded ears off half the number he killed, but he still tried to avoid them whenever possible.

For example, in his two most successful seasons, 1943 and 1944 when he fought a total of 167 corridas, only one of those corridas was with Miuras. It was in Barcelona and that day he cut both ears off both animals, but still he continued to avoid "the miureños"; it was as though he could not forget the fact that the only bull that could rip the life from his great-uncle, the indestructible "Pepete," had been a Miura. He knew Miuras have killed more famous matadors than any other breed, including the great Espartero back in 1898. In 1908 the toreros, led by Bombita and Machaquito, had formed a pact and had refused to fight the "Bulls of Death."

Now here in Linares over in the corrals behind the plaza de toros there awaited six of these dreaded animals. Two of them Manolete would have to kill.

One of the pair was named Islero—Islander.

slero was brought up on the ranch of Eduardo Miura like this calf here, or like any of the others on the big cortijo outside of Sevilla.

His mother, Islera, was "choreada en morcillo"—reddish black with dark stripes—and she charged the horsemen when they came to take the calf in for marking. (Although most fighting bulls are characteristically black, many Miuras are dark or light brown or pinto.)

Even the calf, young as it was, was hard to handle and it tried to charge the horses. Like all toros bravos, it wanted to fight by instinct and years of breeding, not because of any training or goading.

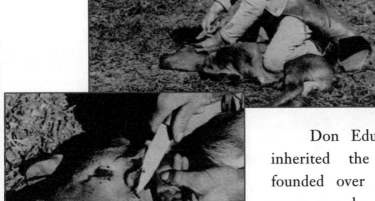

Don Eduardo, who inherited the ganadería founded over a hundred years ago by his great-grandfather, performed the traditional task of notching the left ear of the animal himself.

When he was a yearling, Islero was taken into the corrals and branded with the number 21 on his side and on his flank with the famous ornamental A design. (At the time the breed

was started back in 1848 by Juan Miura the bulk of the males were from the Alvareda ranch). This would be the last time Islero would encounter a dismounted man until Linares.

At two years of age Islero faced the crucial test of his life. Along with the other young males and females, he was tested against a picador. When the animals charged the padded horse, the picador would prick the lance into their withers. The females were graded by how many times and how willingly they charged against this punishment. Some would charge as many as a dozen times and still beg for more; these would be slated for motherhood, because bull breeders say that while a bull inherits its size and strength from his father, he gets his fighting heart from his mother. After their testing, the females were caped by matadors and aspirant matadors for practice, but not the males; if they charged hard and bravely, Don Eduardo called out "toro," made an entry in his notebook on its performance, and it would be slated for the ring someday. If it reacted badly to the pics, he called out "buey" (steer) and the vaqueros immediately cut off its horns, castrated it, and marked it for the abbatoir.

The brave animals were turned out to pasture and for the next years of their life they did nothing but eat and practice using their horns on each other.

Islero went through the stages of growing up—becerro, añojo, eral, utrero, novilla, toro—without incident.

"Out in the country he was a completely ordinary bull," Eduardo Miura wrote me recently. Miura, who took these photographs of his ranch himself, saw absolutely nothing to distinguish Islero from the sixty or so other bulls of his age on the ranch. He was well formed, he was neither too wide nor too closed of horn, he weighed 495 kilos, and he was a Miura.

That was why he was picked this August day, along with five other four year olds, to be shipped to Linares and to be fought by the great Manolete in his duel with Luis Miguel Dominguín. Black and white trained steers helped the herdsmen lead the bulls in from the fields.

They were lured into the corrals, and from there down narrow chutes and into the cajones, or shipping crates.

Once the last crate was loaded, and the big tuck had rattled away from the ranch toward Linares, there was nothing the breeder could do; he'd sit and smoke cigarettes and wait for the important telephone call from his

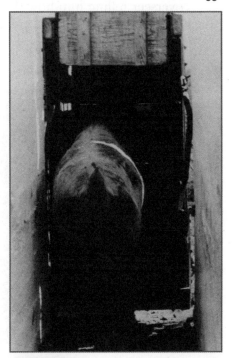

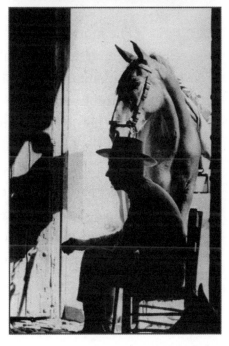

overseer telling him how the animals which he'd raised so carefully for the single purpose of trying to kill men, had done against Spain's two greatest toreros.

The morning of the day of the fight, the matadors' representatives came to the corrals in back of the plaza de toros. They studied the animals carefully and paired them off in the fairest manner possible—the largest animal with the smallest, the most dangerously horned with the least dangerously horned. Then they wrote down the brand numbers of each pair on a cigarette paper, wadded them up, and dropped them in a hat. They covered this with another hat and then the men reached in cautious hands to draw out their matadors' fate.

Some of the bulls fought among themselves as the tense excitement and strange surroundings began to affect them.

But Islero remained calm, almost docile. When it was time to goad them down into the stalls under the stands he went along easily. He would wait for the next few hours in semi-darkness, waiting for the twenty minutes for which all his life had been a preparation.

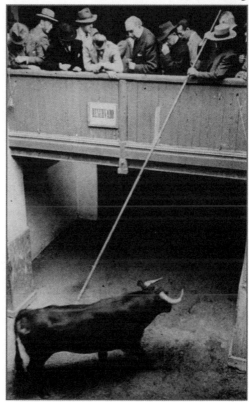

The arena itself was empty now, except for two small boys who played at bullfighting and dreamed of someday being second Manoletes.

In the murkiness of his room at the Hotel Cervantes, Manolete was resting when his manager came in.

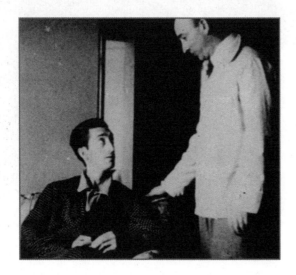

"How are they?" Manolete asked.

"Fine," said Camará. "Not too big, not too small."

Chimo, the second sword handler, arrived and began arranging the equipment and setting out the costume. He reported the conversation with his matador later in the letter to Antonio de la Villa:

"'What suit are you fixing for me?' he asked.

"'The rose one,' I answered. 'See if you can't find me a pair of those stockings that we used to get in Barcelona,' he said, 'because those others wrinkle and with the balls of my feet so sore it bothers me.'

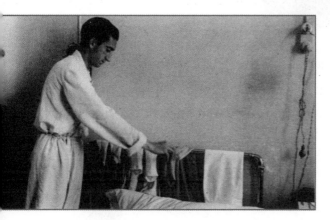

"He went back to sleep, and around 12 I served him lunch. When he sat up I saw a red blotch on his arm like a bite, and smiling I said, 'You must have had some music in here last night.'

"'A Muira got to me sooner than I expected,' answered the matador, smiling; Andalucía has lots of bedbugs and mosquitoes.

"Then he ate a small steak, some grapes, and a cup of coffee. He lit a cigarette and went to the bathroom to wash and shave. At one o'clock, the parade of friends and the curious began; there was his friend the Count of Colombí and the newspaper critic K-Hito, an intimate of his, and

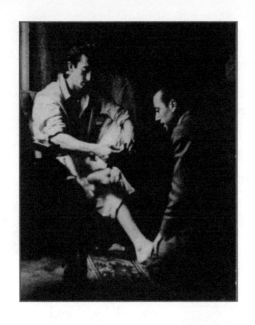

the two of them began to joke. At one point, K-Hito, observing the darkness of Manolete's beard, asked, 'Haven't you shaved yet?'

"'Yes, I've shaved,' said Manolete. 'If my beard's getting darker it's fear that's making the whiskers come out.'

"Carnicerito arrived all dressed. 'Why so soon?' Manolo chided. 'Going to have your portrait painted?' And Manolo kidded him about his amorous weaknesses, which many times had kept him from doing his best with the bulls. Carnicerito had drawn the lots for the bulls that morning and he said that the group of animals weren't too big and seemed manageable enough, judging by the way they let themselves be corralled.

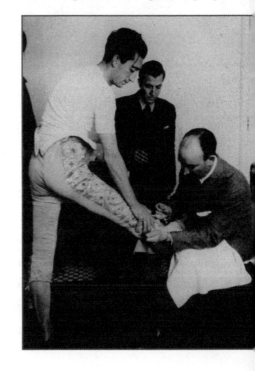

"Then came a newspaperman from the magazine *Life* from America with a photographer and an assistant, and Manolo, smiling said to him, 'We toreros are one person before the fight and another afterwards. If you're looking for a handsomer torero, take the photo after the corrida when the resemblance goes back into place. Fear puts a mask on us now.'"

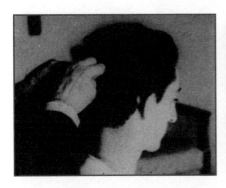
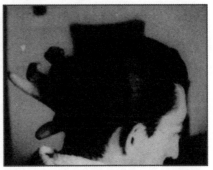

Someone said: "I didn't know you knew what fear was."

Manolete answered: "My knees begin to quake when I sign my name on the contract and they don't stop until the end of the season."

Someone else asked rather pontifically: "Of the many artistic elements in a corrida which is the part of the fight that you find most satisfying?"

Manolete answered wryly: "The part of the drag mules."

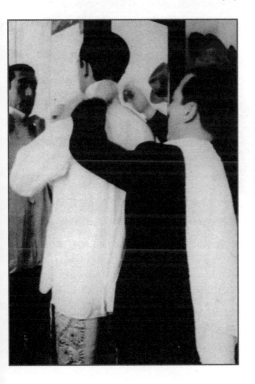
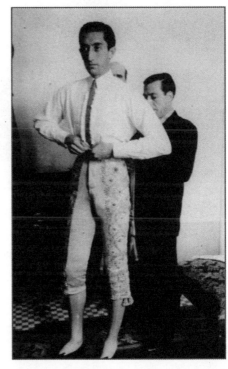

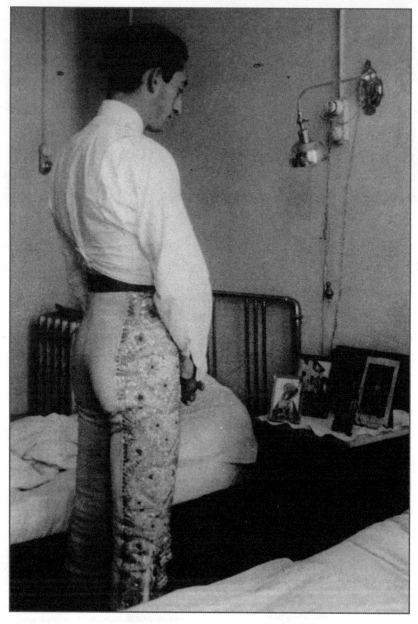

Then he prayed to the Virgen de la Macarena on his night table.

"Virgen mía, please give me luck—don't let them catch me today—protect me once more, I beg of you."

Down the hall in the same hotel, Dominguín was getting dressed. As a sensational young newcomer he had plenty of well-wishers of both sexes.

"You'll show him up" they said, "you're the greatest torero in the world. Manolete is through."

"All I ask is a decent bull," said Dominguín as they helped him into his jacket. "Then I'll prove it to everyone once and for all."

Manolete was almost ready now. The artificial pigtail was on securely, Camará himself had seen that the macho tassels at his knees were not too tight or too loose, and his affairs with the Macarena were in order. Guillermo, the number one sword handler, took the heavy jacket, rose-colored silk encrusted with gold, from the chair.

Then as he, and only he, had done since Manolete was a sixteen-year-old novillero, Guillermo eased Manolete's long arms in the chaquetilla and boosted it up on to his shoulders.

"I want the dress cape with the roses," he said to Chimo. "They always bring us luck."

He folded it under his arm. Then he was as ready as he would ever be. The fight would begin at five-thirty, because of the late summer sun. It was a little after five o'clock already.

"Vámonos," he said.

Some of the toreros, like Manolete's picadors, went to the plaza de toros in carriages. Manolete went in his big custom-made car.

As he pushed his way through the crowd to the back of the ring he stopped to talk to friends who had come from all over Andalucía to see the duel.

Back in the patio de caballos—the horse courtyard—he posed for photographers for last shots.

Some of the bullfighters went into the little chapel to pray.

Others stayed outside, like Dominguín and Manolete, and had a final cigarette.

The two rivals nodded to each other and withdrew to opposite sides of the patio. From within the plaza came the sounds of the gay crowd, the blare of the pasodobles, the shouts of the vendors.

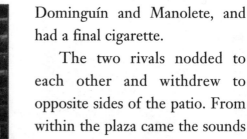

Then the alguacil—the constable —got on his horse and announced with deadly calm: "We might as well start this thing."

It was 5:29. Manolete lined up with his three banderilleros and his two picadors on their horses behind him.

In front were the two alguaciles—dressed in the traditional 16th century costume—ready to lead the parade.

The gate was opened and the crowd cheered in anticipation. Manolete was on the far left, Dominguín in the middle, and Gitanillo de Triana on the right. (Gitanillo, way past his prime, was on the program simply to fill out the bill—in essence the corrida was a "mano-a-mano" between Dominguín and Manolete.)

The band struck up and the parade strode out on the yellow sand.

Manolete walked with his eyes down as usual, with that regal bearing.

When they came to the box of the presidente—the man who would act as judge today—the toreros bowed slightly, the right hand to the montera, and then slid behind the fence.

The sword handlers hurriedly unfolded the big capes, screw-eyed the palillo sticks into the muletas, and got the big sword sheaths ready.

Manolete looked up at the crowd and nodded to some friends up from Sevilla. The trumpet blew for the first bull and since Gitanillo was the oldest matador, it was his animal. Gitanillo did better than expected with the cape and managed to kill the animal quickly. The audience applauded during the performance, but they were impatient; they hadn't come to see Gitanillo.

After Gitanillo's dead bull was dragged out by the mules, the ring was cleared, the trumpet sounded, and Dominguín looked down the fence at Manolete and said: "It's your bull, maestro."

Manolete, his big capote hugged to him, didn't answer as he kept his eyes on the arena.

The toril gate swung open,
and out came the first Miura.

As it charged across the ring, Manolete nodded at one of his banderilleros. "Let's see how he operates."

The man went out and trailing the cape with one hand, he doubled the animal back and forth several times while Manolete studied its style.

Then the peón vaulted the fence and Manolete stepped out quickly from behind the burladero.

He took the animal from the left in a verónica—his hands held low—and the animal skimmed by. But it was not a good bull, it didn't charge hard or honestly, and Manolete quickly saw that there was little to be done with the cape.

With the sword and the muleta in his hand he dedicated the bull to the presidente and then went out for the last part of the performance.

First of all he gave it some wrenching passes de castigo, forcing the bull to charge correctly.

Then he was able to extract a few decent passes from the animal. He even managed to do a few naturals, the pass he had revived in all its classic dignity.

Actually, he extracted a performance from it that no other torero would have attempted.

Standing straight and dignified, he let the bull's horns slice by his legs again and again.

When it came time for the kill he did it as only he knew how. One of the great killers of all history, Manolete simply did not know how to kill a bull in any manner except the straight on, honest, dangerous way, reaching way over and putting the sword in the withers, and at the same time giving the bull a chance to get him.

The first estocada did not kill the bull. The second dropped it immediately.

Some of the crowd applauded but others booed. If it had been any other matador they would have demanded that he be given an ear. But from the great Manolete they expected miracles.

"They keep demanding more and more of me," Manolete complained as they dragged the bull across the ring and out the gate to be butchered, "And I have no more to give."

Camará said, "Maybe your second bull will be better."

"You can beat that," said Dominguín's father from behind the barrera.

"Just let it turn out brave," answered Dominguín. "I'll do the rest."

The Miura came

out hard and fast, and Dominguín quickly saw that it was a good animal to work with. He ran out into the arena and knelt down on the sand with the cape swirled out in front of him.

"Toro, ah hah!" he yelled and when the animal charged, he flipped the cape over his right shoulder.

The animal veered off its course, going up into the air in its eagerness to get the target.

A great roar of "olé" came from the crowd. This is what they had come to see!

The trumpet sounded for the picadors, and the bull charged the padded horse. The picador pricked the bull's neck muscles to lower the massive head for the last third of the fight.

When Dominguín felt that the animal had taken enough punishment he lured the animal away from the horse. Then he did a series of farol passes on his knees.

Each time the animal charged, he pivoted around flashing the cape over his head as he did.

He decided to put in his own banderillas, and grabbing a pair away from his banderillero he ran out into the arena and placed them perfectly in the bull's withers. Two more pair he put in, and each time he let the animal come way into him so that the horns barely missed him.

After dedicating the bull, he started his faena de muleta with three perfect right-hand derechazos.

Then he dropped to his knees and did several hair-raising passes, the bull's horns scraping by his rib cage each time. He had the bull under such control that at one point he could lean forward and kiss the animal on the curly hair between its horns.

Then, knowing from his years of experience that the bull would not charge at that moment, he dropped his sword and muleta and leaned his elbow gingerly on the bull's forehead—"el teléfono."

Kneeling, he turned his back on the bull, holding it by its off horn.

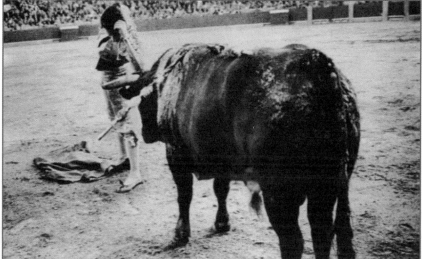

The crowd went wild and already began waving handkerchiefs to indicate to the presidente that he should be granted an ear.

But when it came time to kill, Dominguín had to make three attempts. Finally the sword went in up to the red hilt, and the bull dropped over.

In spite of the bad kill, Dominguín was awarded both ears of the bull, and amidst the admiring glances of the female members of the audience—and cheers of the gallery—he was forced to take two triumphal laps around the arena.

Manolete had smoked a cigarette and watched the performance from the callejón. These circus tricks of Dominguín's were not his idea of what el toreo should be; he believed in serious, classical, honest capework, not crowd-pleasing stunts.

Gitanillo had his second bull to kill and he did it as soon as possible, with little attempt at a faena, knowing he could not compete with Manolete and Dominguín today. As they dragged out the bull Manolete stood up wearily, and got the cape right in his hands—

as the trumpet blew

the "gate of frights clanged open

and out of it slammed Islero,

the last bull of his life,

whirling around and looking for something to kill.

"I need a good bull," said Manolete. "It's about time I had a good bull."

"Well this isn't it," said Camará as he watched the bull charge around the empty ring. "I don't think you're going to like him."

Manolete put on his montera—the lucky hat he had worn since he was a boy, the only montera he had ever owned—and stepped into the ring.

"Double him for me," Manolete ordered his banderilleros. Chimo reported this part of the fight thus:

"Gabriel González and Cantimplas barely doubled the animal at all, and then with great difficulty, because Islero planted himself in the middle of the ring and just stood there wagging his horns wickedly, but with no desire to charge honestly. Manolo called out: 'Quieto, quieto!' to Gabriel.

"Then he opened up his cape and citing with gaiety, he gave
it a verónica
    —and then another the other way,

—and ending with that typical half verónica of his. But he soon saw that Islero was inclined to crowd to the right and hooked badly. Manolo tried again but uselessly since Islero just wouldn't respond. The animal kept putting on the brakes."

Some of the audience appreciated the difficulties of the bull and applauded what Manolete had done. But again many of his detractors booed because he hadn't worked in closer to the animal.

When Manolete came back to the barrera Camará warned: "Let Dominguín have today and take this one wide and safe from now on."

Manolete answered: "We're going to cut ears off this one."

The trumpet blew for the picadors, and when Islero saw the horses come in he prepared to charge.

The picador shook the long vara lance and braced himself.

The bull hit the padded side of the horse square amidships—

—the horse and rider went up in the air

—the picador spilled off onto the bull's back

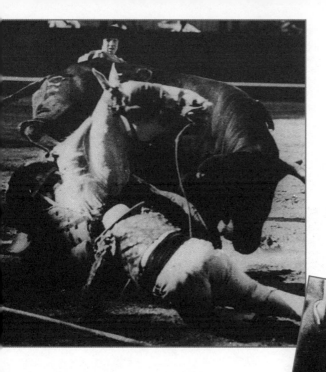

—and then crashed to the ground.

The crowd gasped as they saw the picador helplessly exposed to the bull's horns.

But then Manolete came up fast, flashing his cape in front of the animal and shouting: "Toro, ahaaaaa…"

The bull swung around at the challenging voice and when it charged, Manolete lured it back and away from the picador.

Then, standing perfectly straight, his feet flat on the sand

he swung the cape in a perfect verónica
and the horns passed by only a foot from his body.

The crowd burst into applause, the first solid applause of the day for Manolete.

"We'll make them applaud louder than that," he said as he came to the fence for the sword and muleta.

"No, Manolo!" Camará said. "This one's bad!"

Manolete said: "On the right side we'll make him pass fine."

He walked over in front of the presidente's box, held up his montera, and mouthed the routine request for permission to kill the bull.

Then he wheeled regally and tossed the montera over the fence to the sword handler.

"Echale la mano abajo!" Camará called as Manolete walked out to meet the animal. "Give it to him with your hand low and try to get him under control!"

The banderilleros were in the ring,

having long since realized the animal's dangerous ways and wanting to be near their matador if there was any trouble. But Manolete ordered them out of the ring. "Dejarme solo," he rumbled, "Leave me alone with him!"

Islero charged, and Manolete gave him several low, wrenching "control passes."

Then he stood there straight and unmoving as the animal charged again, and where Dominguín had worked inches away from the bull Manolete dealt in centimeters.

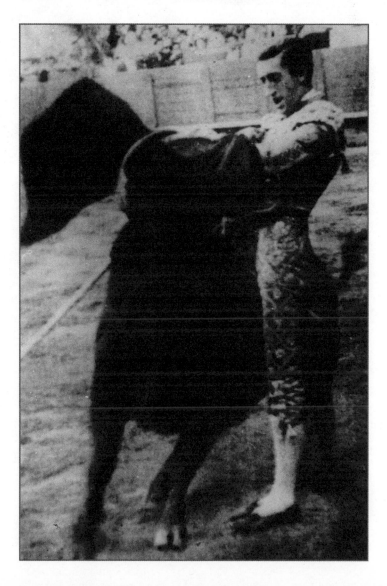

It was the Pass of Death. He followed it with another Pass of Death, watching calmly as the bull followed the muleta.

Then he did one of his rare molinetes, spinning in against the bull's neck as the horn skimmed by his waist.

The crowd was roaring now as he casually looked up at them in the middle of a derechazo

—looking away from death disdainfully as death charged by him again.

Then in the center of the ring, alone in the center of the universe, Manolete held the muleta in the position of the pass he'd given his name to. Catching a bit of the cloth behind his back with his left hand, he spread the muleta with the sword like a mainsail.

"Toro!" he called in his deep voice. "Toma, toro!"

And the bull charged.

"Was it possible to do manoletinas with such a bull?" wrote Cesar Carrasco in the newspapers later, "Yes, it was possible! And what manoletinas! Splendid, exquisite ones which sparkled like the Kohinoor...."

The applause was continuous, spontaneous, sincere, stripped of all prejudice and petty rivalries.

Now Manolete was edging forward across the line of the bull's intended charge. He had the muleta in his left hand, unspread by the sword and hence offering the bull only half the target.

"Toro, ah-haaaa!" The bull was uncertain which to attack, the man's exposed legs or the tantalizing cloth.

But the man made the bull take the rag, made it go for the deception instead of his body—and moving only his wrist, he led the bull around him in a perfect natural, the animal charging as though glued to the folds of the muleta.

"Olé!" came from the crowd in unison.

And then one long continuous "olé!" —as he cited the bull

and wrapped the animal around him

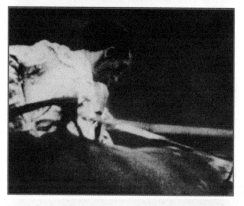

completely around his stationary body

again

and again

and again

and still again

and then he strode away from
the bull.

With his back to death he serenely adjusted the sword in the muleta.

And every man and woman in the audience stood up
to acknowledge the true mastery of the finest craftsman in
his profession.

Then it was time to kill. "Off to the side and fast!" Camará called between cupped hands as Manolete turned and looked over to the barrera.

But Manolete had to end this one correctly, fairly. He "squared" the bull, and then instead of going off to the side and stabbing the bull in the neck the safe way he chose to go in straight over the right horn.

The sword sank into the exact spot between the withers and it looked as though the muleta in his left hand were keeping the bull distracted and on a straight course.

But then Islero hooked to the right suddenly

driving a horn deep into the man's groin.

He was slammed into the air like a manikin

as the crowd screamed.

Islero drove at the fallen man and people watched helplessly.

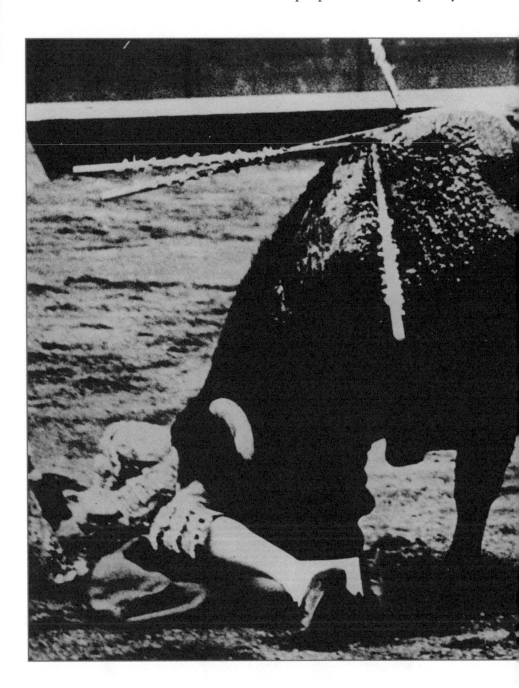

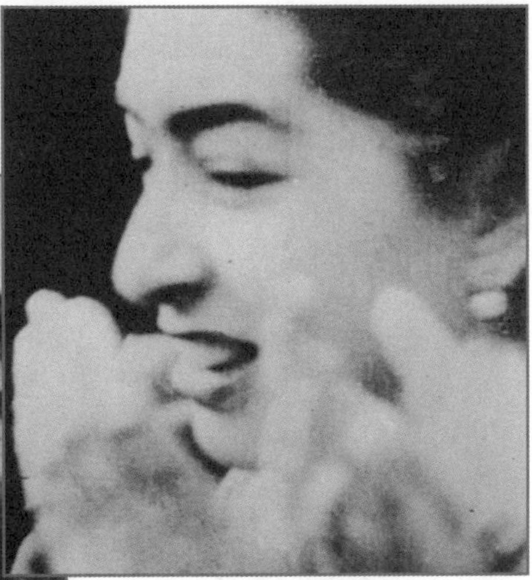

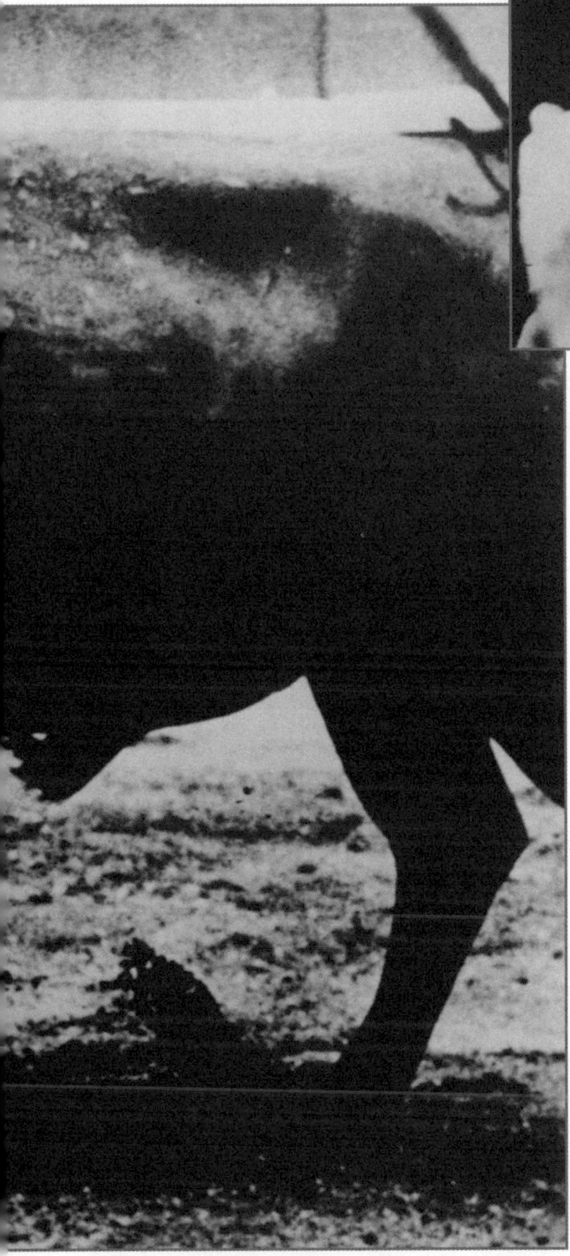

The bull was distracted away for a moment as Manolete's helpers ran to rescue him, but then the stunned crowd saw it whirl back at its victim.

He lay crumpled underneath the bull's back legs as one of the banderilleros grabbed its tail and another looked as though he

would strangle the animal with his bare hands. Frantically grabbing Islero by the horns and flashing capes before it, they kept it occupied while a monosabio dragged the matador from under the animal's feet.

They hastily picked the man up and started for the infirmary, getting the wrong door twice.

Before they found the correct one, the bull Islero had dropped dead of the sword thrust.

The people in the stands sat tense, silent and guilty with the shock of the cornada. Was it as bad as it looked? There were two pools of blood, two enormous pools black on the sand.

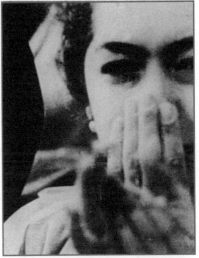

The trumpet sounded and the toril gate swung open again. They'd forgotten; there was still another bull. Dominguín was the Número Uno now, and he went out to show that he deserved the title. But few people paid any attention to what was going on in the ring. *Did we kill that man?* some were thinking. *Yes, we helped kill that man.*

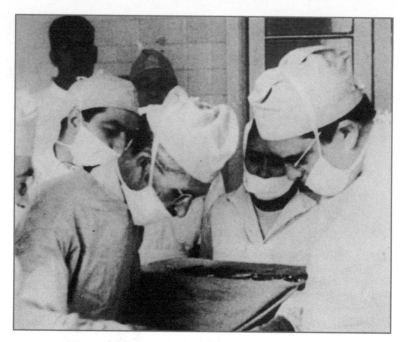

Manolete was in a state of shock when he arrived at the ring infirmary. As the doctors slashed off his uniform and began to give him a transfusion, a banderillero came in with the ears and tail of the bull which the presidente had granted.

The operation lasted forty minutes. At eight o'clock he came to. The members of his cuadrilla and Camará stood around him.

"Ay, put my leg better," he moaned, "It feels doubled up under me."

At eight-thirty, he was given another transfusion.

At nine-thirty, they put him on a stretcher and carried him across the darkening arena to the nearby hospital where the facilities were better.

Manolete said over and over: "Slow—slow, God, the pain, the pain!"

In the hospital another transfusion was given to him and the doctors reexamined the wound.

Around midnight Manolete suddenly raised his head and said: "Did the bull die?"

"Yes, Manolo," Camará answered, tears streaming down his face. "Lie back now."

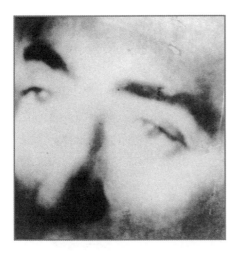

"You mean it died," Manolete exclaimed, "and they didn't even give me anything?"

"They gave you everything," said Camará. "Both ears and the tail."

Manolete lay back with a little smile.

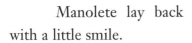

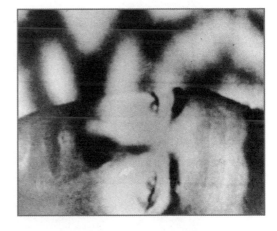

At two o'clock, Jiménez Guinea, the top horn wound specialist in Spain, arrived from Madrid. Jiménez Guinea held a consultation with the other doctors, agreed with what had been done, and decided not to touch the wound but to concentrate on keeping up Manolete's weakening pulse.

Upon seeing the doctor, Manolete took heart. But then he said anxiously: "Don Luis, aren't you even going to look at the wound?"

"You rest now, Manolo," he answered, "and we'll look at it in the morning."

Antoñita Bronchalo arrived from Lanjarón, but it was thought best that she didn't go in. The emotion might be too much for him.

A priest was called and he was given the Extreme Unction.

At five o'clock, he said, "Don Luis, I can't feel anything in my right leg."

"You'll be all right, Manolo," the doctor soothed.

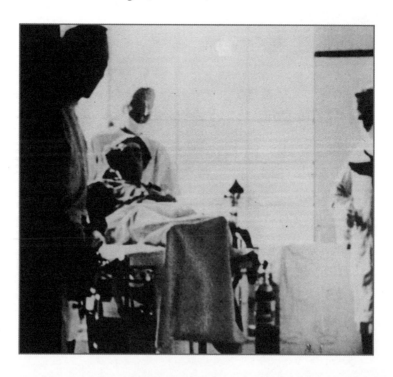

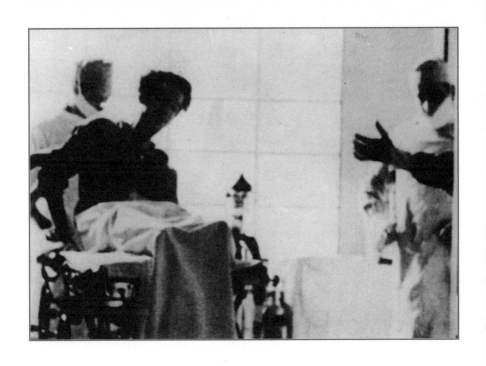

"Don Luis, I can't feel anything in my left leg!"
"Lie back Manolo," said the doctor.

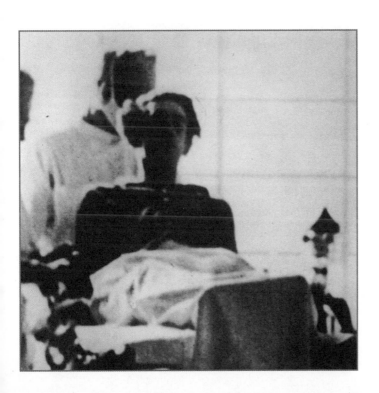

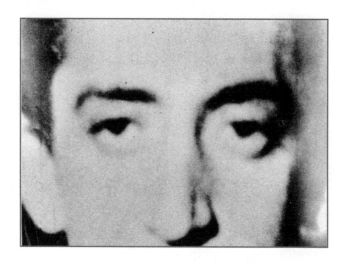

Manolete sat bolt upright. "Doctor, are my eyes open?

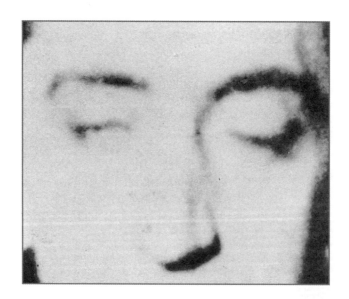

I can't see!"

He fell back dead.

Camará could only stare numbly at the body of his friend as they folded the dead man's hands around the crucifix.

Now Antoñita was allowed in. She flung herself on the body and she would stay there for the next six hours, unmindful, unaware, of the stream of people who began to come into the room to pay their last respects to Manolete. One of them was Dominguín, who, stunned and with tears in his eyes, pressed his cheek against the dead man's hands.

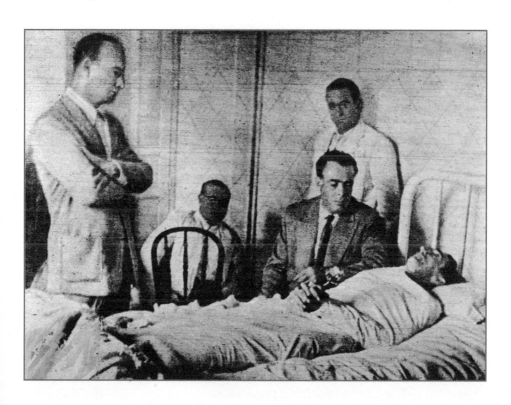

A shocked Spain was already reading about the death of Manolete. Every Spaniard, whether a duke or a shoeshine boy, deeply felt that part of Spain and part of himself had

died with Manuel Rodríguez. Yet at the same time they felt a guilty thrill at the drama of his death, the Spanishness, the archaistic poetry of it.

"He killed dying and he died killing," said one newspaper.

Manolete's body was taken back to Córdoba. Thousands of mourning people filed past in the two days that the body lay in state.

Camará sat off in the shadows alone, silent, forlorn, wondering how he was going to go on with half of his being missing.

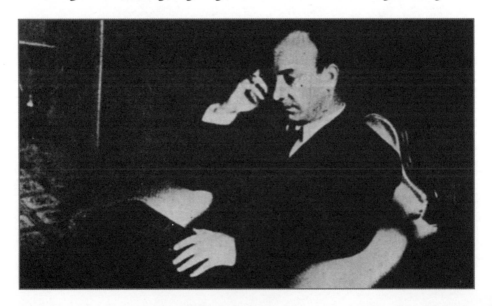

Manolete's funeral was the largest ever witnessed in Spain. People came from all over the country to attend it, just the way they had come to see him confront Dominguín in Linares. He had won against Dominguín, he had conquered all Spain, all the world, but the price was expensive. Now he had come home, very tired.

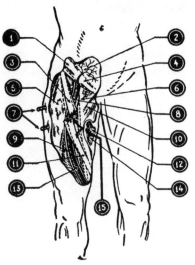

Una explicación de la forma en que se desarrolló la intervención quirúrgica

El doctor D. Rafael Blanco León, nos ha facilitado el esquema de la herida que publicamos, debido a que se encontró presente en la segunda intervención quirúrgica que sufrió el diestro.

Como complemento del dibujo, nos permitimos describir la herida, ateniéndonos al parte facultativo que se dió en la enfermería de la plaza de Linares.

El asta del toro penetró por la cara interna de la pierna derecha, al nivel del vértice del triángulo Scarpa, que está formado por los músculos Sartorio, arco crural, y primer aductor. Dicha región que aloja el paquete vásculo-nervioso, está integrado por el nervio crural, las arterias y vena femoral y por la base del citado triángulo, la safena, mucho más superficial.

En la trayectoria hacia arriba lesionó al mismo tiempo el músculo recto anterior del abdomen y las arterias subcutáneas abdominales. Como esta era una herida encubierta por la piel, después de ligar la Safena, continuarían sangrando las abdominales, por lo que hubo que escindir la piel para proceder a la ligadura de los vasos.

En la trayectoria hacia abajo, rompió, además del Sartorio, el recto anterior que sufrió desgarraduras, en sus fibras musculares, así como también quedó rota la arteria que riega este músculo y que es derivación de la arteria femoral, la cual sale debajo de la femoral profunda, causa del trauma, todo el paquete vásculonervioso quedó traumatizado y desplazado hacia su parte externa.

Una gran vascularización de pequeñas venas y arteriolas riegan la masa muscular de dicha región, imposible muchas veces de ligar en su totalidad. Aunque queden sin ligar estas pequeñas arteriolas no ponen en peligro la vida del paciente, pero en los recovecos de la herida suelen quedar depositados algunos coágulos que más tarde pueden producir infecciones. Para dar salida a estos coágulos y exudados que se ocasionaran, el cirujano hizo dos aberturas en la cara externa del muslo, colocando tubos de drenaje. A su vez se aplicaron a la herida polvos de sulfamidas (polvos de Azol) —que tantas infecciones evitan— y se preparó la penicilina por si se hacía necesaria. La herida quedó abierta y los tubos de drenaje fueron retirados después de la segunda intervención.

Los doctores, desde el primer momento, se dieron cuenta de la gravedad extrema del herido y por la pérdida de sangre sufrida se hacían necesarias transfusiones sanguíneas, para las cuales se ofrecieron muchos de los presente. No obstante a todos estos medios heróicos empleados para salvar su vida, el schock continuaba, el pulso seguía cada vez más débil, el corazón insuficiente y fatalmente llegó su hora final por la falta de reacción en las pulsaciones y su insuficiencia cardiaca. El fuerte schock hizo fallar —desgraciadamente— los elementos quirúrgicos y médicos que se emplearon.

The newspapers of the world relished the death of Manolete. In the usually conservative Spanish papers, there was little about anything else for a week. There were interviews with his doctors, lugubrious chats with members of his family and his cuadrilla, the last impressions of the concierge in the hotel where he had stayed, every taurine expert's opinion on how and why the tragedy had occurred, and even detailed diagrams of the actual wound that killed him.

The rest of the world was interested but more restrained. The British *Daily Express* headlined: "World's Champion Bullfighter Killed." The New York newspapers told about "the millionaire toreador" on their front pages. *Time* Magazine said, in part:

"Anglo-Saxons who (without His express consent) had elected God to the board of directors of the SPCA would never understand why men stood weeping...on Mexico street corners. Or why the altars in private homes were draped in black. Or why jammed movie theaters cancelled feature pictures to show, over and over, movies of a man whose name most Anglo-Saxons had never heard.... Throughout the Spanish world plain people felt they had lost one who had given them not joy, but a bitter glorious excitement, a pageant of death and courage, death's enemy...."

Genereal Franco posthumously awarded Manolete La Cruz de la Beneficencia, Spain's highest civilian decoration. Letters of condolence came from all over the world, from the Prime Minister of England, from poor people, rich people, hod carriers, lawyers, writers, artists, and diplomats.

They read the letters to Manolete's mother, twice widowed and now bereft of her favorite child, and tried to console the old woman who was trying to find a reason for continuing to live.

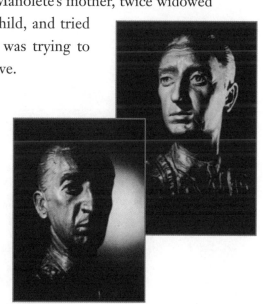

Now came the honors accorded departed royalty: from the death mask there followed heroic, glorified busts, full length statues, and hundreds of paintings.

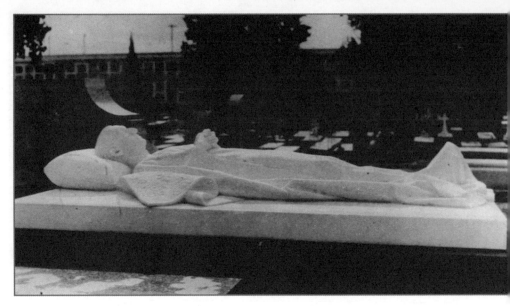

Over the grave there was erected a marble tomb that dwarfs all others in the Córdoba graveyard. Stretched full length in a marble shroud, his dress cape beneath his shoulders, Manolete lies serenely at the feet of a large crucifix.

The sculptor has accentuated his romanesque features, and some poets, referring to the days when Córdoba belonged to Rome, spoke of Manolete as a fallen Caesar and compared his glories to those of the ancient Seneca and Lucan, fellow Cordovans.

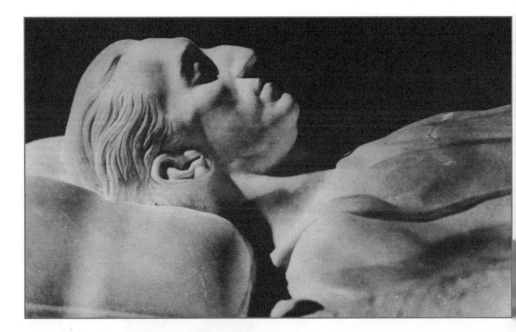

Two years after his death, a committee headed by Carlos Arruza raised a million pesetas by giving a benefit bullfight to erect a giant monument to Manolete in the city of Córdoba. Every top-flight poet in Spain wrote a threnody for the occasion, but none could compete with the statement of one of his banderilleros who, with tears in his eyes, had looked at his matador's body shortly after his death and said:

"They kept demanding more and more of him, and more was his life, so he gave it to them."

Manolete's Performances

FROM THE YEAR HE BECAME
A FULL MATADOR UNTIL HIS DEATH

SEASON OF 1939

Date	City	Fellow Performers	Trophies
3–19	Córdoba	Gallito, Luis Díez	
4–9	Córdoba	Calderón, Martin Vázquez	1 ear
5–14	Sevilla	Revertito, Yoni	1 ear
5–21	Sevilla	Fernandi, Martín Vázquez	
5–26	Córdoba	Revertito, Calderón	
5–28	Córdoba	López Lago, Martín Vázquez, Fernandi	
6–8	Cádiz	Sánchez Mejías, Calderón	1 ear
6–12	Algeciras	Pepe Luis Vázquez, Paquito Casado	2 ears and tail
6–18	Algeciras	Pepe Luis, Calderón	
6–24	Cabra	Pepe Luis, Casado	1 ear
6–25	P. S. María	Gallito, Casado	3 ears and tail
7–2	Sevilla	Chicuelo, Gitanillo de Triana	2 ears (takes alternative)
7–18	Sevilla	Niño de la Palma, P. Bienvenida	
7–30	P. S. María	Domingo Ortega, Pascual Márquez	4 ears, 2 tails
8–13	Algeciras	Pepe Bienvenida, La Serna	
8–15	Jaén	Chicuelo (hand to hand)	
8–27	S. Sebastián	P. Bienvenida, Márquez	2 ears and tail
9–4	Málaga	Niño de la Palma, P. Bienvenida	
9–10	S. Sebastián	La Serna, El Estudiante	
9–12	Valladolid	Ortega, Juanito Belmonte	
9–24	Valladolid	Rafaelillo, El Estudiante	
10–1	Barcelona	Chicuelo, Belmonte, Curro Caro	2 ears and tail
10–8	Barcelona	Chicuelo, Caro	
10–12	Madrid	Juan Belmonte, Sr. Lalanda, Juanito Belmonte	2 ears and tail (confirms alternative)
10–13	Zaragoza	Vicente Barrera, Jaime Noain	
10–15	Madrid	Cañero, Belmonte, Lalanda, P. Bienvenida	(rained out)
10–16	Zaragoza	P. Bienvenida, El Estudiante	
10–17	Madrid	Cañero, Belmonte, Lalanda, P. Bienvenida	(rained out)
4–7	Barcelona	Ortega, Belmonte	2 ears and tail

SEASON OF 1940

Date	City	Fellow Performers	Trophies
4-14	Barcelona	Lalanda, V. Barrera	
4-18	Sevilla	Ortega, Márquez	2 ears
4-19	Sevilla	Ortega, Belmonte	
4-20	Sevilla	Márquez, Belmonte	1 ear
4-28	Barcelona	Chicuelo, P. Bienvenida	2 ears
5-5	Barcelona	Lalanda, Caro	
5-12	Zaragoza	El Estudiante, Pericás	
5-12	Cádiz	Gallardo, Belmonte	
5-23	Córdoba	Ortega, Rafaelillo	2 ears
5-25	Madrid	Lalanda, V. Barrera, Ortega	2 ears
6-9	Algeciras	Chicuelo, Ortega	
6-10	Algeciras	V. Barrera, Ortega	
6-13	Madrid	Ortega, Mariano García	
6-16	Castellón	Ortega, Belmonte	2 ears
6-19	Bilbao	Ortega, Belmonte	
6-23	Alicante	Ortega, P. Bienvenida	
6-24	Alicante	Lalanda, Ortega	2 ears and tail
6-29	Burgos	Ortega, P. Bienvenida	
6-30	Burgos	Ortega, Belmonte	
7-4	Madrid	Ortega, Rafaelillo, Belmonte	
7-5	Bilbao	Lalanda, V. Barrera, Ortega, El Estudiante, Belmonte	(Festival)
7-7	Pamplona	Caro, Belmonte	
7-9	Pamplona	Ortega, P. Bienvenida	
7-10	Pamplona	Ortega, Belmonte	
7-14	Madrid	Ortega (hand to hand)	
7-18	Murcia	Ortega (hand to hand)	4 ears, 2 tails
7-22	Madrid	Lalanda, Ortega, P. Bienvenida, Belmonte, Mariano García	(Festival)
7-25	Valencia	Ortega, P. Bienvenida	
7-26	Valencia	Lalanda, V. Barrera, P. Bienvenida	(gored)
7-30	Valencia	V. Barrera, Ortega	
8-1	Valencia	Ortega (hand to hand)	
8-4	Santander	Lalanda, Ortega	
8-11	Málaga	Ortega (hand to hand)	
8-12	Málaga	Niño de la Palma, Ortega	
8-15	S. Sebastián	Lalanda, Ortega, Belmonte	2 ears and tail
8-18	Bilbao	V. Barrera, Belmonte	
8-22	Bilbao	Ortega, Belmonte	2 ears
8-25	S. Sebastián	Rafaelillo, Belmonte	
9-1	Granada	Ortega (hand to hand)	2 ears and tail
9-3	Priego	Niño de la Palma, Ortega	
9-5	Ubeda	Niño de la Palma, Ortega	
9-8	Murcia	Ortega, Pepe Luis	
9-10	Albacete	Lalanda, Ortega, P. Bienvenida	2 ears and tail
9-11	Albacete	Rafaelillo, Belmonte, Casado	
9-12	Salamanca	Ortega, Casado	
9-13	Salamanca	Lalanda, Ortega, Pepe Luis	
9-15	Valladolid	Ortega, Casado	

Date	*City*	*Fellow Performers*	*Trophies*
9–16	Valladolid	Lalanda, Ortega, Pepe Luis	
9–25	Córdoba	Lalanda, Ortega	
10–6	Valencia	V. Barrera, Ortega	2 ears and tail
10–20	Jaén	Ortega, P. Bienvenida	4 ears, 2 tails

SEASON OF 1941

3–16	Valencia	Lalanda, Pericás	2 ears and tail
3–30	Barcelona	V. Barrera, P. Bienvenida, La Serna	2 ears and tail
4–3	Madrid	Lalanda, P. Bienvenida, La Serna, Belmonte, Pepe Luis, Gallito	2 ears
4–6	Barcelona	Chicuelo, Caro	(slight wound)
4–18	Sevilla	Belmonte, Pepe Luis	2 ears
4–19	Sevilla	P. Bienvenida, Pepe Luis	
4–20	Sevilla	P. Bienvenida, Belmonte, Pepe Luis	2 ears and tail
4–27	Barcelona	Pericás, Belmonte, Gallito	
5–4	Barcelona	P. Bienvenida, Belmonte	2 ears, tail, 1 hoof
5–18	Barcelona	Ortega, P. Bienvenida, Belmonte	
5–22	Barcelona	Belmonte, Gallito	(slight wound in shoulder)
5–25	Córdoba	Belmonte, Gallito	
5–26	Córdoba	Chicuelo, Pepe Luis	
6–1	Barcelona	V. Barrera, P. Bienvenida	
6–2	Barcelona	Lalanda (hand to hand)	
6–8	Algeciras	P. Bienvenida, Pepe Luis	
6–9	Plasencia	Gitanillo de Triana, Gallito	
6–12	Granada	Lalanda, Gallito	1 ear
6–15	Barcelona	Lalanda (hand to hand)	3 ears, tail, 1 hoof
6–22	Barcelona	Lalanda, V. Barrera, Belmonte, Pepe Luis, Gallito	
6–29	Lisboa	Rafaelillo	
7–6	Barcelona	Pepe Luis, Martín Vázquez	1 ear
7–13	Barcelona	Lalanda (hand to hand)	2 ears, tail, 1 hoof
7–18	Barcelona	V. Barrera, Pericás	1 ear
7–20	P. Mallorca	V. Barrera, Pericás, Belmonte	
7–25	Valencia	P. Bienvenida, P. Barrera	2 ears
7–26	Valencia	Lalanda, P. Bienvenida, Belmonte	2 ears and tail
7–27	Barcelona	Ortega, P. Bienvenida, Pepe Luis	
7–31	Valencia	Lalanda, Martín Vázquez	
8–3	Vitoria	V. Barrera, Gallito	2 ears and tail
8–5	Vitoria	Lalanda, Belmonte, Pepe Luis	2 ears
8–10	Málaga	Lalanda, Pepe Luis	
8–13	Baeza	Casado, Sánchez Mejías	
8–15	Barcelona	Rafaelillo, Casado, P. Barrera	2 ears and tail
8–17	Bilbao	V. Barrera, Pepe Luis	
8–18	Bilbao	P. Bienvenida, Belmonte	
8–19	Toledo	Lalanda (hand to hand)	2 ears
8–21	Antequera	Cagancho, Casado	
8–24	Bilbao	V. Barrera, Belmonte	2 ears and tail
8–26	Almagro	Lalanda (hand to hand)	2 ears and tail
8–29	Linares	Lalanda, Pepe Luis	4 ears

Date	City	Fellow Performers	Trophies
8–31	Barcelona	Cagancho, P. Bienvenida	
9–3	Mérida	V. Barrera, Casado	2 ears
9–7	Murcia	Belmonte, Pepe Luis	
9–8	Murcia	Belmonte, Pepe Luis, P. Berrera	(cheek wound)
9–22	Logroño	V. Barrera, Gallito	(leg injury)
9–23	Logroño	Pepe Luis, Gallito	(leg injury)
9–26	Córdoba	Lalanda, Pepe Luis	2 ears
9–28	Madrid	Lalanda (hand to hand)	
10–1	Madrid	Lalanda, Martín Vázquez	
10–5	Zafra	Casado (hand to hand)	
10–9	Madrid	Lalanda, P. Bienvenida, P. Barrera	2 ears
10–12	Barcelona	Lalanda, P. Bienvenida, Pepe Luis	2 ears and tail
10–14	Zaragoza	Rafaelillo, Gallito	
10–16	Zaragoza	Villalta, Gallito	1 ear
10–18	Jaén	Pepe Luis, Martín Vázquez	
10–19	Jaén	P. Bienvenida, Pepe Luis	2 ears and tail

SEASON OF 1942

Date	City	Fellow Performers	Trophies
3–15	Barcelona	Pepe Luis (hand to hand)	
3–18	Valencia	V. Barrera, P. Bienvenida, Pepe Luis	
3–19	Valencia	Belmonte, V. Barrera	
3–29	Barcelona	Belmonte, Pepe Luis, Andaluz	1 ear
4–5	Zaragoza	Pepe Luis, Andaluz	
4–6	Barcelona	V. Barrera, Pepe Luis, Andaluz	(kills 3 bulls after Berrera's injury)
4–12	Barcelona	P. Bienvenida, Pepe Luis, Martín Vázquez	
4–18	Sevilla	Pepe Luis, Andaluz	
4–19	Sevilla	Pepe Luis, Gallito	
4–20	Sevilla	Pepe Luis, Gallito	
4–21	Sevilla	Pepe Luis, Gallito, Andaluz	
4–26	Andújar	Pepe Luis (hand to hand)	(rained out)
4–30	Jerez	Pepe Luis, Casado	
5–3	Alicante	Belmonte, Sánchez Mejías, V. Barrera	2 ears and tail
5–10	Valencia	V. Barrera, Belmonte	2 ears, tail, 1 hoof
5–14	Barcelona	Pepe Luis, M. Talavera	2 ears
5–25	Córdoba	Belmonte, Pepe Luis	4 ears, 2 tails
5–26	Córdoba	P. Bienvenida, Pepe Luis	
5–27	Córdoba	Pepe Luis, Martín Vázquez, Andaluz	
5–31	Cáceres	Pepe Luis, M. Talavera	2 ears and tail
6–4	Granada	Pepe Luis, Martín Vázquez	
6–7	Granada	Belmonte, Pepe Luis	
6–14	Algeciras	Pepe Luis, Casado	2 ears and tail
6–15	Algeciras	Pepe Luis, Andaluz	
6–19	Bilbao	Pepe Luis, A. Bienvenida	2 ears and tail
6–21	Barcelona	P. Bienvenida, Pepe Luis, M. Talavera	4 ears, 2 tails
6–24	Badajoz	Belmonte, Pepe Luis, Casado	
6–28	Barcelona	Lalanda, P. Bienvenida	
6–29	Barcelona	Lalanda, Villalta	2 ears and tail
7–5	Barcelona	Villalta, Belmonte	2 ears

Date	City	Fellow Performers	Trophies
7–7	Pamplona	P. Barrera, Andaluz	
7–9	Pamplona	Belmonte, Martín Vázquez	
7–10	Pamplona	Pepe Luis, Andaluz	
7–12	Barcelona	Pepe Luis, A. Bienvenida, M. Talavera	
7–16	S. Fernando	Gallardo, Casado	
7–18	Sevilla	Chicuelo, Pepe Luis	
7–19	Huelva	Pepe Luis, Casado	
7–23	Valencia	P. Bienvenida, Belmonte, M. Talavera	4 ears, 2 tails
7–24	Valencia	V. Barrera, Belmonte	2 ears, tail, 2 hoofs
7–25	Barcelona	P. Bienvenida, Belmonte	2 ears, tail, 1 hoof
7–26	Barcelona	Chicuelo, Villalta, P. Bienvenida, Pepe Luis, A. Bienvenida	4 ears, 2 tails
7–27	Valencia	V. Barrera, Andaluz	3 ears, tail, 1 hoof
8–2	Vitoria	El Estudiante, Andaluz	2 ears and tail
8–3	Coruña	M. Talavera, L. M. Dominguín	2 ears and tail
8–5	Vitoria	Gallito, Andaluz, M. Talavera	2 ears and tail
8–9	Santander	Niño de la Palma, Pepe Luis	2 ears and tail
8–13	Baeza	Pepe Luis, Casado	
8–15	S. Sebastián	Belmonte, Pepe Luis, Andaluz	2 ears
8–17	S. Sebastián	Pepe Luis, M. Talavera	
8–19	Bilbao	Pepe Luis, Gallito	2 ears
8–20	Toledo	Ortega (hand to hand)	2 ears
8–26	Cieza	Martín Vázquez, Andaluz	
8–27	Almería	Pepe Luis, Casado	2 ears
8–28	Linares	P. Bienvenida, Pepe Luis	2 ears, tail, 1 hoof
8–29	Constantina	Casado, Martín Vázquez	2 ears and tail
8–30	P. S. María	Chicuelo, Martín Vázquez	2 ears, tail, 1 hoof
9–3	Mérida	Belmonte, M. Talavera	
9–4	Aranjuez	Ortega, M. Talavera	4 ears, 2 tails, 1 hoof
9–6	Barcelona	Belmonte, Pepe Luis, Andaluz	2 ears, tail, 1 hoof
9–8	Murcia	Belmonte, Pepe Luis, P. Barrera	
9–9	Villanueva del Arzobispo	P. Bienvenida, Martín Vázquez	4 ears
9–10	Albacete	Ortega, Belmonte, Pepe Luis	2 ears
9–11	Albacete	P. Bienvenida, Pepe Luis	2 ears
9–12	Salamanca	Lalanda, Pepe Luis, Juan Mari	2 ears and tail
9–13	Salamanca	Ortega, Belmonte, Pepe Luis	
9–17	Madrid	Belmonte (hand to hand)	
9–20	Valladolid	Ortega, Pepe Luis	2 ears and tail
9–21	Valladolid	Lalanda, Belmonte, Pepe Luis	2 ears and tail
9–23	Logroño	Pepe Luis, Andaluz, M. Talavera	4 ears, 2 tails, 1 hoof
9–24	Barcelona	Lalanda, P. Bienvenida, Belmonte	2 ears and tail
9–26	Quintanar	Ortega, Luis Ortega	1 ear
9–27	Madrid	Belmonte, Gallito	(gravely wounded)

SEASON OF 1943

Date	City	Fellow Performers	Trophies
3–19	Barcelona	A. Bienvenida, M. Talavera	
3–21	Barcelona	P. Bienvenida, Juan Mari	2 ears, tail, 1 hoof
3–28	Castellón	Belmonte, Pepe Luis	(gravely wounded)
4–25	Barcelona	Pepe Luis, M. Talavera	

Date	City	Fellow Performers	Trophies
4–26	Barcelona	Belmonte, Juan Mari	
5–2	Murcia	P. Barrera, Manuel Escudero	2 ears and tail
5–9	Barcelona	Morenito Valencia, A. Bienvenida	2 ears
5–16	Valencia	Belmonte, Juan Mari	1 ear
5–23	Barcelona	Chicuelo, M. Valencia	
5–25	Córdoba	Gallito, M. Talavera	1 ear
5–26	Córdoba	P. Bienvenida, Juanito Belmonte	2 ears and tail
5–27	Córdoba	Chicuelo, Belmonte, M. Talavera	
5–28	Córdoba	Chicuelo, P. Bienvenida, Belmonte, Gallito, M. Talavera	
5–29	Madrid	Belmonte, M. Escudero	1 ear
5–30	Madrid	Chicuelo, L. M. Dominguín	
5–31	Teruel	Gallito, El Estudiante	2 ears
6–2	Madrid	Belmonte, A. Bienvenida, M. Talavera	1 ear and tail
6–9	Plasencia	Belmonte, M. Talavera	
6–10	Madrid	Belmonte, M. Talavera	
6–13	Algeciras	Pepe Luis, Valencia III	1 ear
6–14	Algeciras	Pepe Luis, Miguel del Pino	
6–19	Bilbao	Pepe Luis, A. Bienvenida	1 ear and tail
6–21	Bilbao	Pepe Luis, M. Talavera	2 ears
6–25	Badajoz	P. Bienvenida, Andaluz	1 ear
6–26	Badajoz	Belmonte, M. Talavera	2 ears
6–27	Granada	Pepe Luis, M. Talavera	
6–28	Alicante	A. Bienvenida, M. Escudero	4 ears, 2 tails, 2 hoofs
6–29	Alicante	A. Bienvenida, Martín Vázquez, Andaluz	2 ears and tail
7–4	P. Mallorca	Pepe Luis, Andaluz	2 ears and tail
7–7	Pamplona	P. Bienvenida, Julián Marín	2 ears and tail
7–8	Pamplona	Pepe Luis, Marín	2 ears and tail
7–9	Pamplona	Pepe Luis, A. Bienvenida	2 ears, tail, 1 hoof
7–10	Pamplona	Pepe, Antonio and Angel Luis Bienvenida, Pepe Luis, Marín	(Festival)
7–11	Madrid	Belmonte, Escudero	2 ears and tail
7–13	Bilbao	Cagancho, El Estudiante, Pepe Luis, Gallito, A. Bienvenida	2 ears and tail
7–15	Madrid	Pepe Luis, Juan Mari, Pérez Tabernero	1 ear and tail
7–18	Barcelona	Martín Vázquez, A. Bienvenida	1 ear and tail
7–21	Valencia	P. Bienvenida, Pepe Luis, Andaluz	
7–23	Valencia	Pepe Luis, Valencia III	1 ear and tail
7–24	Valencia	P. Bienvenida, Belmonte, Martín Vázquez	
7–26	Valencia	El Estudiante, Marín	
7–27	Valencia	Belmonte, Casado	
8–1	Santander	Belmonte, M. Talavera	1 ear and tail
8–3	Coruña	Belmonte, L. M. Dominguín	4 ears, 2 tails
8–5	Vitoria	Belmonte, Juan Mari	2 ears
8–6	Vitoria	El Estudiante, M. Talavera	
8–8	Santander	Andaluz, Juan Mari	
8–10	Huesca	El Estudiante, M. Talavera	
8–13	Baeza	P. Bienvenida, Belmonte	1 ear and tail
8–15	P. S. María	Andaluz, M. del Pino	(gored in right leg)
8–27	Almería	P. Barrera, M. Talavera	1 ear and tail

Date	City	Fellow Performers	Trophies
8–28	Linares	P. Barrera, M. Talavera	1 ear and tail
8–29	Linares	P. Bienvenida, Belmonte	
8–30	Soria	P. Bienvenida, Marín	
8–31	Calahorra	P. Bienvenida, El Estudiante	1 ear and tail
9–2	Palencia	Pepe Luis, M. Talavera	
9–3	Mérida	Belmonte, Pepe Luis	
9–4	Priego de Cord	Belmonte, P. Barrera	2 ears and tail
9–5	Cuenca	Belmonte, M. Talavera	
9–6	Burgos	Pepe Luis, Escudero	
9–7	Burgos	Pepe Luis, Belmonte	2 ears and tail
9–8	Murcia	P. Barrera, A. Bienvenida, Escudero	4 ears, 2 tails
9–10	Albacete	P. Bienvenida, Pepe Luis, Andaluz	
9–11	Albacete	Belmonte, Pepe Luis	(gored in right thigh)
9–21	Logroño	Andaluz, M. Talavera	4 ears (gored by 2nd bull)
9–22	Logroño	El Estudiante, Pepe Luis	2 ears
9–28	Oviedo	Simao da Veiga, Belmonte	
10–1	Barcelona	P. Bienvenida, Belmonte, Andaluz	1 ear
10–3	Hellín	P. Bienvenida, Belmonte	1 ear
10–4	Ubeda	P. Bienvenida, Andaluz	
10–6	Caravaca	P. Barrera (hand to hand)	2 ears
10–10	Barcelona	M. Escudero, Angelete	
10–13	Zaragoza	El Estudiante, Pepe Luis	1 ear
10–15	Zaragoza	Pepe Luis, M. Talavera	4 ears
10–17	Zaragoza	Villalta, M. Talavera	2 ears
10–18	Jaén	Ortega, Gallito	
10–19	Jaén	Ortega, Casado	2 ears

SEASON OF 1944

Date	City	Fellow Performers	Trophies
3–18	Valencia	Pepe Luis, Martín Vázquez	2 ears
3–19	Valencia	Andaluz, Valencia III	2 ears
4–8	Cartagena	Belmonte, Juan Mari	
4–9	Zaragoza	V. Barrera, Pepe Luis	
4–19	Sevilla	El Estudiante, Pepe Luis	4 ears
4–20	Sevilla	Pepe Luis, Andaluz	
4–23	Barcelona	Belmonte, Juan Mari	
4–30	Jerez	P. Bienvenida, M. del Pino	
5–7	Sevilla	Domecq, Pepe Luis, Andaluz	
5–14	Barcelona	Belmonte, M. Valencia	1 ear
5–21	Zaragoza	El Estudiante, Belmonte	
5–25	Córdoba	Domecq, P. Bienvenida, Juan Mari	3 ears and tail
5–26	Córdoba	Belmonte, M. Valencia	
5–28	Barcelona	Domecq, Pepe Luis, Albaicín	3 ears and tail
5–29	Barcelona	Domecq, V. Barrera, M. Valencia	
5–30	Cáceres	M. Talavera, Angelete	1 ear
5–31	Cáceres	Ortega, Pepe Luis	
6–1	Madrid	Domecq, El Estudiante, Andaluz, A. L. Bienvenida	1 ear
6–4	Lisboa	Nuncio, M. Talavera, Arruza	Symbolic Ears

Date	City	Fellow Performers	Trophies
6–8	Granada	Ortega, Casado	1 ear
6–11	Algeciras	Ortega, Pepe Luis	1 ear
6–12	Algeciras	Ortega, Pepe Luis	1 ear
6–15	Barcelona	Domecq, Ortega, D. Dominguín	4 ears
6–18	Bilbao	El Estudiante, Andaluz	1 ear
6–19	Bilbao	Ortega, El Estudiante	
6–22	Madrid	El Estudiante, Pepe Luis	3 ears
6–24	Alicante	Belmonte, Andaluz	4 ears
6–27	Barcelona	Ortega, Gitanillo de Triana	
6–28	Alicante	Andaluz, A. L. Bienvenida	
6–30	Burgos	P. Bienvenida, Andaluz	1 ear
7–2	Barcelona	Veiga, Ortega, Andaluz	4 ears
7–6	Madrid	El Estudiante, Belmonte	3 ears
7–16	La Línea	V. Barrera, P. Dominguín	2 ears and tail
7–19	Lisboa	Ortega, Fermín Rívera	
7–21	Valencia	Ortega, Belmonte	3 ears
7–22	Valencia	V. Barrera, Belmonte, Andaluz	
7–23	Valencia	Andaluz, A. Bienvenida	2 ears and tail
7–24	Valencia	Domecq, El Estudiante, Belmonte	
7–25	Tudela	Ortega, El Estudiante	2 ears and tail
7–28	Valencia	Domecq, Belmonte, Andaluz	1 ear
8–4	Vitoria	Ortega, Juan Mari	1 ear
8–5	Vitoria	El Estudiante, Belmonte	
8–6	Santander	Ortega, A. L. Bienvenida	2 ears
8–9	Málaga	Ortega, El Estudiante	4 ears
8–10	Málaga	Chicuelo, Ortega	
8–11	Manzanares	El Estudiante, Pepe Luis	2 ears
8–13	Santander	Belmonte, M. Valencia	1 ear
8–14	S. Sebastián	Ortega, Pepe Luis	1 ear
8–15	S. Sebastián	El Estudiante, Pepe Luis, Juan Mari	2 ears and tail
8–17	Lisboa	Casimiro, El Estudiante, El Soldado	
8–20	Gijón	Ortega, Pepe Luis	(gored)
8–21	Bilbao	P. Bienvenida, Valencia III	4 ears
8–23	Bilbao	P. Bienvenida, Andaluz	
8–23	Bilbao	Ortega, Belmonte	
8–25	Almería	Ortega, L. M. Dominguín	4 ears, 2 tails
8–26	Cieza	P. Bienvenida, Arruza	3 ears and tail
8–27	P. S. María	Ortega, Del Pino	2 ears and tail
8–29	Linares	Ortega, P. Bienvenida	2 ears and tail
8–30	Linares	Domecq, El Estudiante, Pepe Luis	
8–31	Cádiz	Domecq, Ortega, Arruza	2 ears and tail
9–2	Palencia	El Estudiante, Juan Mari	4 ears, 1 tail
9–3	Mérida	El Estudiante, Belmonte	4 ears, 2 tails
9–4	Aranjuez	El Estudiante, Rivera	
9–5	Cuenca	Gitanillo, Belmonte	4 ears
9–6	Cuenca	Ortega, El Estudiante	
9–7	Villanuevi del Arzobispo	El Estudiante, Arruza	
9–8	Murcia	Belmonte, Andaluz	
9–9	Calatayud	El Estudiante, P. Bienvenida	
9–10	Zamora	F. Domínguez, L. M. Dominguín	

Date	City	Fellow Performers	Trophies
9–12	Salamanca	Ortega, Pepe Luis	
9–13	Salamanca	Pepe Luis, Andaluz, Juan Mari	
9–14	Ceheguín	Ortega, Martín Vázquez	2 ears and tail
9–15	Madrid	Belmonte, A. Bienvenida	
9–16	Oviedo	Belmonte, Arruza	2 ears and tail
9–17	Valladolid	El Estudiante, Arruza, Andaluz	2 ears and tail
9–18	Valladolid	Ortega, Pepe Luis	
9–21	Logroño	Pepe Luis, Arruza	4 ears, 2 tails
9–22	Logroño	El Estudiante, Arruza	3 ears, 2 tails, 1 hoof
9–23	Logroño	El Estudiante, Pepe Luis	4 ears
9–28	Madrid	Domecq, Gitanilla, El Soldado	1 ear
9–30	Hellín	Ortega, El Estudiante	1 ear
10–1	Hellín	P. Bienvenida, Belmonte	3 ears and tail
10–5	Zafra	Ortega (hand to hand)	2 ears and tail
10–8	Murcia	Rivera, Niño del Barrio	2 ears
10–12	Alicante	El Estudiante, Rivera, L. M. Dominguín	4 ears
10–14	Zaragoza	El Estudiante, Pepe Luis	2 ears and tail
10–15	Valencia	Andaluz, Choni	3 ears and tail
10–16	Zaragoza	Ortega, El Estudiante	3 ears and tail
10–17	Zaragoza	Ortega, Rivera	1 ear
10–18	Jaén	Ortega, Martín Vázquez	2 ears and tail
10–19	Jaén	Ortega, Rivera	
10–29	Gerona	Domecq, P. Bienvenida, Caro	2 ears and tail

SEASON OF 1945

Date	City	Fellow Performers	Trophies
3–17	Valencia	Andaluz, Choni, Veiga	2 ears
3–18	Valencia	Rivera, Choni	
3–19	Valencia	El Estudiante, Rivera	2 ears
4–1	Zaragoza	El Estudiante, Arruza	
4–15	Murcia	Arruza, Andaluz	
4–18	Sevilla	Arruza, Pepe Luis	2 ears
4–19	Sevilla	Arruza, Martín Vázquez	1 ear
4–20	Sevilla	P. Bienvenida, Pepe Luis	2 ears
4–21	Sevilla	Rivera, Pepe Luis	2 ears
5–3	Coruña	Caro, Arruza	1 ear
5–4	Coruña	Arruza, Pepe Luis	1 ear
5–5	Coruña	Gitanillo, Rivera, Veiga, Domecq	2 ears and tail
5–6	Alicante	Arruza, Martín Vázquez	
5–9	Valencia	Arruza, Parrita	4 ears, 2 tails, 1 hoof
5–10	Barcelona	Arruza, Martín Vázquez	
5–13	Lisboa	Armillita, Rivera	
5–17	Barcelona	Arruza, Parrita	4 ears
5–20	Barcelona	Ortega, Parrita	1 ear
5–21	Barcelona	Ortega, Carnicerito de México, Parrita	3 ears
5–30	Madrid	Armillita, Ortega, Parrita	
5–31	Toledo	Arruza, Parrita	2 ears, tail, 1 hoof
6–1	Granada	Martín Vázquez, Parrita	2 ears, tail, 1 hoof
6–2	Granada	Ortega, Arruza	
6–3	Granada	Arruza, Martín Vázquez	2 ears and tail
6–6	Barcelona	Arruza, Gitanillo de Triana	4 ears, tail, 1 hoof
6–9	Plasencia	Arruza, Pepe Luis	4 ears and tail

Date	City	Fellow Performers	Trophies
6–10	Plasencia	Domecq, Ortega, Dominguín	
6–14	Madrid	Pepe Luis, L. M. Dominguín	
6–17	Bilbao	Armillita, Pepe Luis	
6–18	Bilbao	Pepe Luis (hand to hand)	2 ears
6–19	Bilbao	Armillita, L. M. Dominguín	
6–23	Badajoz	Caro, Arruza	4 ears, 2 tails
6–24	Alicante	Arruza, Choni, Domecq	2 ears and tail
6–27	Barcelona	Arruza (hand to hand)	2 ears
6–29	Alicante	P. Bienvenida, Arruza, Parrita	2 ears and tail (clavicle broken)
8–6	Vitoria	Arruza, Martín Vázquez	2 ears
8–28	Linares	Arruza, Parrita	2 ears and tail
8–29	Linares	Arruza, Martín Vázquez	
8–30	Barcelona	Arruza, Llorente	2 ears and tail
8–31	Barcelona	Arruza (hand to hand)	2 ears and tail
9–2	Santander	El Estudiante, Arruza	2 ears
9–3	Gijón	Armillita, Parrita	
9–7	Toledo	Arruza, Parrita	2 ears
9–8	Murcia	Arruza, Parrita, Veiga	3 ears and tail
9–9	Murcia	Arruza, P. Bienvenida, Domecq	2 ears and tail
9–10	Albacete	Ortega, Arruza, Domecq	2 ears and tail
9–11	Albacete	Arruza, Martin Vázquez	
9–12	Albacete	Arruza, L. M. Dominguín, M. Talavera	
9–13	Salamanca	Ortega, Rivera	
9–14	Salamanca	Pepe Luis, Arruza	2 ears
9–16	Barcelona	P. Bienvenida, Marín, Llorente	2 ears
9–17	Valladolid	Ortega, Arruza	2 ears
9–18	Valladolid	Pepe Luis, Arruza	2 ears
9–20	Lisboa	Arruza (hand to hand)	
9–21	Logroño	Arruza (hand to hand)	
9–22	Logroño	Arruza, Martín Vázquez	
9–23	Barcelona	Ortega, Arruza, Domecq	
9–24	Barcelona	Arruza, Marín, Parrita, Domecq	2 ears and tail
9–25	Barcelona	Ortega, Arruza, Choni, Veiga	2 ears
9–26	Barcelona	Arruza (hand to hand)	2 ears
9–29	Ubeda	Arruza, Martín Vázquez	4 ears
9–30	Hellín	Arruza (hand to hand)	4 ears, 2 tails, 2 hoofs
10–1	Hellín	Arruza, Parrita	
10–5	Zafra	Arruza (hand to hand)	
10–6	Valencia	P. Bienvenida, Arruza, Correira	2 ears
10–7	Valencia	Arruza (hand to hand)	1 ear
10–12	Barcelona	Ortega, Velázquez	2 ears and tail
10–13	Barcelona	Ortega, Parrita	2 ears and tail
10–14	Zaragoza	Ortega, Carnicerito de México	2 ears, 2 tails, 1 hoof
10–15	Zaragoza	Ortega, Rivera	
10–16	Zaragoza	Rivera, Andaluz	1 ear

SEASON OF 1946

| 9–19 | Madrid | Domecq, Gitanillo, A. Bienvenida, L. M. Dominguín | 1 ear |

SEASON OF 1947

Date	City	Fellow Performers	Trophies
6–22	Barcelona	Belmonte, Boni	2 ears and tail
6–24	Badajoz	Caro, Parrita	
6–26	Segovia	Gitanillo de Triana, Parrita	
6–29	Alicante	Gitanillo de Triana, Caro	1 ear
7–3	Lisboa	L. M. Dominguín, Parrita	1 ear
7–6	Barcelona	Gitanillo de Triana, Marin	2 ears
7–10	Pamplona	Gitanillo de Triana, Martín Vázquez	4 ears
7–13	La Línea	Cagancho, Gitanillo de Triana	3 ears and tail
7–16	Madrid	Gitanillo de Triana, Martín Vázquez	2 ears (wounded in leg)
8–4	Vitoria	Gitanillo de Triana, Parrita	2 ears
8–5	Vitoria	Belmonte, L. M. Dominguín	1 ear
8–6	Santander	Gitanillo de Triana, Martín Vázquez	2 ears and tail
8–8	Valdepeñas	Caro, Martín Vázquez	2 ears and tail
8–10	S. Sebastián	Gitanillo de Triana, M. Navarro	
8–11	Huesca	Belmonte, Paco Muñoz	2 ears
8–15	Gijón	Belmonte, Muñoz	2 ears
8–16	S. Sebastián	Belmonte, L. M. Dominguín	2 ears
8–17	Toledo	Gitanillo de Triana, Muñoz	
8–24	Gijón	Gitanillo de Triana, Parrita	
8–26	Santander	Belmonte, Rovira	
8–28	LINARES	GITANILLO DE TRIANA, L. M. DOMINGUÍN	2 EARS AND TAIL

In addition to these corridas, Manolete fought 31 times in 1946 in Mexico, Colombia, Venezuela and Peru. The end of 1946 and the beginning of 1947 saw him performing 22 times in Latin America.

He usually performed in half a dozen charity fights each year in addition to those listed here.

As a novillero, Manolete fought in 68 novilladas from 1931 until his alternative in 1939.

Credits for Photographs